GRANT GUSTAFSON
THE ART OF GUITAR
BEGINNING CLASS METHOD

Teacher's Edition

Introduction

The Art of Guitar **Beginning Class Method** offers a complete introductory guitar course for classroom or studio instruction. It will guide students to an understanding of how the different elements of music fit together, as well as seeking to instill in them the joys of making music with others. The preferred instrument is the nylon string "classic" guitar and the playing technique is the one universally associated with this type of guitar. It offers a basis for advancing to any other playing style on any other type of guitar.

From day one, students begin to develop the skills to communicate through music. Notes and chords are introduced in the context of guitar-friendly keys and scale passages, which allows for a clearer comprehension of their meaning. Music, representing diverse cultures and styles, is divided into melody, chords, and bass lines, in order to be better analyzed and appreciated. Music is also written in the three basic forms of guitar music notation—staff, tablature, and chord charts—to accommodate different learning styles.

The Teacher's Edition is meant to supplement your lesson planning. It will offer suggestions, but you are encouraged to find other sources of creativity and inspiration. Find other appropriate songs, make your own arrangements, or create your own compositions. Ask your students for suggestions, such as contemporary music they would like to play. Above all, let music making be fun.

Dedicated to my wife, Lory.

Acknowledgments

My heartfelt appreciation goes out to my students, colleagues, teachers, friends, and family throughout the world, who have inspired in me a love for sharing the art of playing the guitar. In preparation of the present edition, I particularly wish to thank: Lory Ann Darnell for *To Get Back*, and for her constant support and encouragement; Michael Fitzgerald, for his aphorisms; all at Sidwell Friends School; and Laurel Plapp and Chuck Elledge for their editorial assistance and valuable suggestions.

ISBN 0-8497-5517-4

kjos NEIL A. KJOS MUSIC COMPANY, PUBLISHER

TABLE OF CONTENTS

USING *THE ART OF GUITAR* BEGINNING CLASS METHOD, TEACHER'S EDITION

The Teacher's Edition of *The Art of Guitar* Beginning Class Method provides **Teacher Tips, Activities, Interdisciplinary Studies, Worksheets,** and **Quizzes** to supplement your lesson planning. This information is provided on "teacher pages." For easy reference, each "teacher page" precedes or faces the corresponding page(s) from the student edition, which have been reproduced in black and white.

Teacher Tips provide an overview of the material in the lesson and ways to introduce new techniques and music theory. Additional Teacher's Edition **Activities** can be used to supplement those provided in the student book. **Teacher Tips** and **Activities** that are located in shaded boxes are essential for reinforcing the basic concepts of music theory and guitar performance presented in each lesson.

Recommended **Warm-up** activities on selected teacher pages provide exercises to prepare students for the new material in the lesson of the day. Each class period should begin with a warm-up, including tuning, simple finger exercises, scales, and/or familiar songs. At the end of each class period, help students wind down by playing a favorite song, or performing the new song or exercise learned in the lesson of the day.

Interdisciplinary Studies present relevant historical, geographical, and cultural information for specially chosen songs throughout the book. Understanding the historical and social context in which the work was composed will greatly enhance students' musical experience. These sections can be read aloud to students in class, or can be used as inspiration for supplementary activities or discussions in class.

Seven duplicable **Worksheets** are provided in the back of the Teacher's Edition (pages 138–144), which are correlated with specific pages in the student edition. Each worksheet is designed to reinforce or expand upon new material, and several of the worksheets contain composition and in-class ear training activities.

A duplicable **Evaluation Worksheet** (page 159) is intended to be used as an in-class group activity at any point in the course beginning in Unit 6. After students have mastered a particular piece, duplicate and distribute the worksheet, and have students divide into groups of five. Each student will first perform the scale and chord progression appropriate for the musical selection, and then the musical selection itself. The other students in the group will evaluate the performance based on the criteria provided.

Twelve duplicable **Quizzes** (pages 145–157) are correlated with the last page of each unit (Units 2 and 3, and Units 13 and 14 have joint quizzes). These quizzes test students on all essential new material covered in the unit. Students may complete them in class or as a homework assignment.

Teacher Tips, Student pages 2–3:

• Student pages 2 and 3 introduce students to a variety of guitar types and styles of guitar music. These pages can serve as an ongoing reference throughout the course.

• Explain the goals of the course and what students will have achieved by the end. Although the final recital will be the culmination of the course, the purpose is to learn basic guitar-playing skills and to enjoy making music with others.

Activities, Student pages 2–3:

• Ask each student what his or her prior musical experience is and what they wish to gain from the course. This is valuable information not only to you, but also to fellow students.

• Read to students the introduction to guitars on student page 2.

• Once students have studied the guitar illustrations, have them complete the *Famous Guitarists* exercise on student page 3. Ask students to name their favorite guitarists and guitar recordings. Encourage students to share experiences they have had with guitars, such as attending a concert or meeting a guitarist.

• Play recorded examples of different guitar styles, and ask students to write down their impressions of these styles. This activity should be continued throughout the course. Ask students to consider the following questions after they have heard recordings of two or three different guitar styles:

  1. How are similar feelings expressed in different styles of music?

  2. How is the guitar used to express these feelings?

  3. For more advanced students: which time signatures are prevalent?

• Keep a current events bulletin board with clippings on guitar styles, music, and concerts. Divide the board into the styles listed on student pages 2 and 3. Have students identify these styles and make connections between instruments, styles, and guitarists.

Worksheet 1, Student pages 2–3:

• The duplicable Worksheet 1 is provided on page 138. Worksheet 1 is an overview of the history of the guitar, with lists of guitarists associated with each type of guitar. As the course progresses, require students to complete a short research paper (500 words) on one of the guitarists listed on Worksheet 1, or one of their own choosing. Provide students with several weeks to complete the assignment, and have them present their papers in class.

1– INTRODUCING: THE GUITAR!

When Christopher Columbus sailed to the New World in the late 15th century, he brought with him a guitar. It was the first musical instrument to reach the Americas from Europe. Although guitars of that era were small and delicate, the guitar has evolved over the past 500 years into many different types as it has been adopted by various cultures and musical styles.

Most guitars still in use today developed from the "classic" guitar, an acoustic (non-electric), six-string instrument which originated in Spain in the 19th century. Spanish designers further modified this guitar to fit the needs of flamenco, the spirited folk music of Spain, by adding a plate on the top which performers tap to make percussive sounds.

In the 20th century, steel strings were introduced in North America, which led to the creation of the "western" guitar. American designers, searching for a way to better project the sound of the guitar, also created the electric guitar. This guitar became essential to rock and jazz.

Learning to play the "classic" guitar will give you a good foundation for starting to play other types of guitars, and will introduce you to the vast world of music available to the guitar player.

Nylon String Acoustic Guitar ("Classic" Guitar)

Styles:
Classical, Latin American, folk, jazz, flamenco

Famous Guitarists:
Andrés Segovia, Charlie Byrd, Sharon Isbin, Paco de Lucia, Agustín Barrios Mangoré

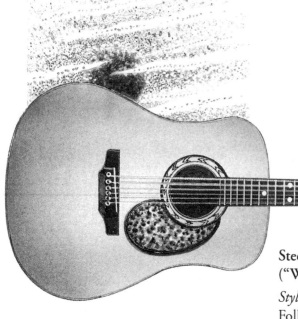

Steel String Acoustic Guitar ("Western" Guitar)

Styles:
Folk, bluegrass, country, blues

Famous Guitarists:
Joni Mitchell, Woody Guthrie

12-string Acoustic Guitar

Style:
Blues

Famous Guitarists:
Leo Kottke, Leadbelly

**Electric Guitar
(solid body)**

Styles:
Rock, blues, country, jazz

Famous Guitarists:
B. B. King, Les Paul,
Eric Clapton, Jimi Hendrix,
Bonnie Raitt

Electric Guitar (hollow body)

Styles:
Jazz, country

Famous Guitarists:
Joe Pass, Django Reinhardt

Famous Guitarists

On the lines below, write the names of other well-known guitarists and what type of guitar each uses. Share an experience with your class about a guitar concert you attended, a guitarist you have met, or a recording that you have heard.

_____

_____

Teacher Tip, Student page 4:

• To provide students with the opportunity to interact with their guitars right away, have students turn to *Experiment! Be Creative!* on student page 6. This activity allows the students to create an initial emotional relationship with the guitar and discover some of its characteristics by themselves.

Activities, Student page 4:

• Read to students the information on the structure of guitars provided on student page 4.

• Review the parts of the guitar with students, pointing them out on your guitar.

• Have students quiz one another on the names of the parts of the guitar and their functions.

• Provide students with unlined paper and pencils. Have students look at a guitar from all angles for 60 seconds. Then, remove the guitar from view, and have them draw the guitar from memory.

• Discuss how sound is made on the guitar. Some students may believe that the vibrations of the strings enter the guitar through the soundhole. However, sound is produced when the vibrating string causes the saddle and then the soundboard to vibrate. In order to demonstrate this for students, place your hand over the saddle, and pluck a string to show that the sound does not resonate when the saddle is not vibrating.

• Discuss the bracing system beneath the soundboard and how vibrations are distributed to create an even sound (without the braces, the bass tones would be loud and the treble would be inaudible).

• Explain to students that different types of woods are used for different parts of the guitar: soft woods (cedar, spruce) for the top, hardwoods (rosewood, mahogany, walnut, maple, fruit woods, ebony) for the back, sides, and neck. Explain to students that the tone quality of a guitar is determined in part by the types of woods used in making the guitar. Laminated plywoods are an inexpensive and more durable alternative to the solid woods mentioned above, but the tone quality is not as full and rich.

• To help students understand the difference between steel and nylon strings, play recordings of music performed on steel string guitars and on nylon string guitars. Ask students to identify the differences in tone, such as the brightness of steel strings and the warmth of nylon strings. Steel strings have much more tension than nylon, so if they are put on a nylon string guitar, they will pull the instrument apart.

• Demonstrate how to place the guitar into a hard-shell case:
Hold up the top of the case when placing or removing the guitar so that the metal latches do not fall onto the guitar. Never sit or stand on the guitar case. Always close at least one latch when putting the guitar in its case. Otherwise, the guitar might fall out when the case is picked up.

All guitars have basically the same shape, and the parts commonly share the same names. Acoustic guitars are generally made of thinly cut, fine-grain woods. The hollow body of the acoustic guitar is what amplifies (increases) the sound. When a string is played, it causes the entire instrument to vibrate, creating natural amplification. A bracing system inside the guitar helps distribute the vibration throughout the instrument for the best tone.

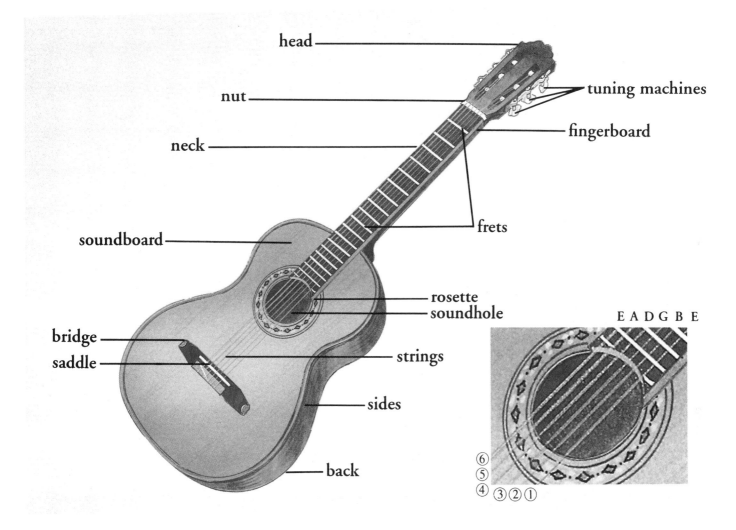

 Naming the Guitar Parts

Find each item listed below on your guitar, and check off each term as you find it. Use the diagram above to help you.

- ☐ head
- ☐ nut
- ☐ sides
- ☐ bridge
- ☐ frets
- ☐ soundhole
- ☐ saddle
- ☐ back
- ☐ fingerboard
- ☐ neck
- ☐ soundboard
- ☐ rosette
- ☐ tuning machines
- ☐ strings

Keep your guitar in its case when it's not being played. Do not store your guitar near a heating source or in a damp place because the wood of the guitar is fragile and can be easily cracked or damaged.

Teacher Tips, Student page 5:

- Tuning the strings of an instrument requires focus and sensitivity. At the beginning of the course, have the instruments pre-tuned. Compare your strings with each individual student's strings, and let them hear differences and make adjustments if necessary. Do not spend too much time on mastering the skills of tuning. Sensitivity will develop over time.

- If you wish students to learn to tune their own guitars, instructions and a diagram are provided on student page 72. Demonstrate the steps in the tuning process for students. For further tips on tuning and tuning activities, refer to page 136.

Activities, Student page 5:

- Review the names and numbers of the strings with students.

- Define the term "pitch" as the highness or lowness of a sound.

- Explain to students that "up is down and down is up." This means that the strings with the highest pitch are close to the ground and the strings with the lowest pitch are furthest from the ground when the guitar is held correctly.

- Have students play their strings once they are in tune to hear how the guitar sounds when in tune. Then, put one of the strings on your guitar out of tune and have students identify the un-tuned string by comparison with their own guitars. Once they have identified the un-tuned string, ask them whether it needs to be tuned higher or lower.

- Have students choose partners and create a six-word phrase, each word beginning with the letter name of a string. Draw a vertical fingerboard on the chalkboard for reference. Students may be confused that the phrase progresses from left to right, while the strings are numbered from right to left.

- Help students develop the ability to recognize tones by completing an activity like the ones described below.

  Play all six strings from bass to treble. Then, play a single string and say the number of that string. Ask individual students to name this string.

  Play all six strings from bass to treble. Then, play one of the strings, without saying the number, and ask a student to identify it by sound (without looking). That student can repeat the process for another student in the room until all have tried. To simplify: Select two or three distant strings from which to choose (low E, middle G, high E). Continue using this exercise during the first weeks of the course. Add new tones as you progress. This listening exercise can be expanded to include two or three tones, different rhythms, and short phrases.

The thick metal wound strings on the guitar produce the lowest pitches or sounds. The thin nylon strings produce the highest pitches. Each string on the guitar has both a letter name (E, A, D, G, B, or E) and a number name (⑥, ⑤, ④, ③, ②, or ①). The strings can be tuned to the correct pitch by adjusting the tuning machines. Ask your teacher for assistance in tuning. (Instructions for tuning your guitar by yourself are provided on page 72.)

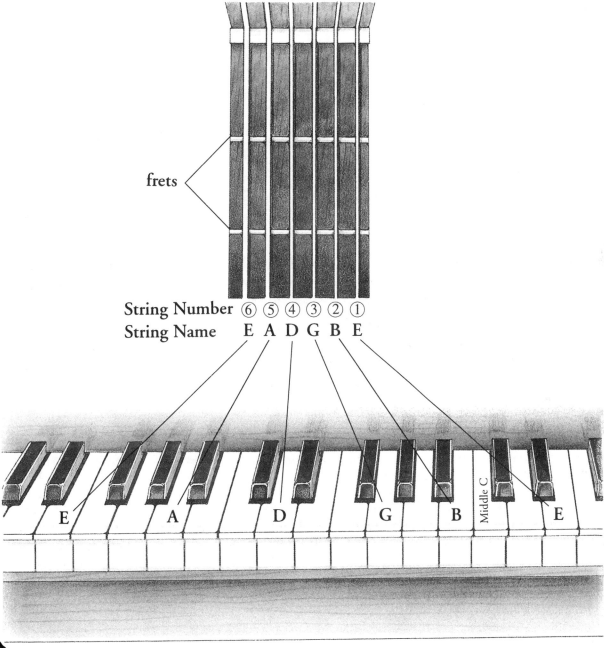

frets

String Number ⑥ ⑤ ④ ③ ② ①
String Name   E A D G B E

E   A   D   G   B   Middle C   E

 Memory Game

Memorize the letter and number names of the strings. With a partner, think of a phrase or statement that will help you remember the names of the strings, and write it on the lines below.

_____

_____

Teacher Tip, Student page 6:

- The *Experiment! Be Creative!* activity and the activities below will help students become familiar with the guitar and with each other. Remind students, as they complete these activities, that they should treat their guitars with sensitivity, without banging or striking their instruments with other objects.

Activities, Student page 6:

- Share with students that percussive sounds on the guitar are used in the music of many cultures of the world, especially in Latin America, and in modern guitar compositions.

- Have students complete the *Experiment! Be Creative!* activity either in partners or individually. This activity prepares students for understanding musical notation. Once students have recorded their sounds in the boxes on student page 6, have each student perform their sound(s). Have the class invent their own symbols for the performer's sounds and compare.

- *Come together.* Each student finds a sound and plays it at his or her own speed (**tempo**) and loudness (**dynamic**). At a signal, they should merge together and find a common beat and dynamic. At another signal, they should go their own way again. Try the activity again without signals, letting the group decide when to merge without using words or other signs.

- *Coming closer… moving away.* Complete the activity above, but have students focus on getting louder (**crescendo**) and getting softer (**decrescendo**), both as they play their own music and as they play in a common beat. Let students give the signals, and then try the activity without signals.

- *Sound machine.* Each student finds a different sound. Go around the circle with each playing his or her sound one after the other. Do this with a consistent beat. Have students experience speeding up and slowing down.

- *Catch.* In a circle, one student plays a sound and non-verbally tosses it to another student. This student catches it and tosses it further. Variations: a) The sound is changed with each toss. b) Maintain a steady beat. c) Change the beat. d) Maintain a steady rhythm. e) Change the rhythm.

- *Storytelling.* Divide the class into smaller groups. Have them create background sounds to a story. Or, have the groups create a story without words, only using sounds. Let the other students in the class guess what is being expressed. Students should not play melodies ("skilled" guitarists should not be at an advantage).

- *Dialogue.* Divide the class into pairs. Let them speak musically to one another through sounds. Such as: a) One student makes a statement and the other responds either with a similar mood or an opposite. Then switch roles and repeat. b) Create an ongoing conversation. c) Try speaking together.

- *Moods.* Have students express different moods through sounds. Let the class guess which moods are being expressed.

- Complete the Unit 1 Review checklist at the bottom of student page 6 with students.

Unit 1 Quiz, Student page 6:

- The duplicable Unit 1 Quiz is provided on page 145. The quiz tests students on the parts of the guitar, names of the strings, types of guitars, and styles of guitar music.

Experiment! Be Creative!

Even if you do not know how to play a single note, you can make music on the guitar right away. Experiment with different sounds on the guitar: snap the strings, tap the side of the guitar with your fingertips, or run your fingers up and down the strings. Create as many unique sounds as you can. Make up a story with the sounds you find, and share your discoveries with your class or a partner.

Invent symbols for the sounds you create and draw them in the empty boxes. Use the example shown in number 1 for inspiration.

1.

1. Striking the back of the guitar like a bongo drum. Louder sounds are shown as larger dots.

2.

2. _____

3.

3. _____

4.

4. _____

Unit 1 Review

☐ history of the guitar   ☐ parts of the guitar
☐ types of guitars   ☐ letter names/number names of the strings
☐ styles of guitar music

Teacher Tips, Student page 7:

- Most students will initially select the "folk" position. However, the "classic" position is good for advanced playing since it allows easier access to the upper playing positions on the fingerboard.

- Cut a 4 x 4 into 6-inch long blocks to be used as footrests. These can be used as a support for both positions. In the "folk" position, the footrest will be under the right leg. Alternatives to the blocks include innovations such as: the adjustable guitar footstool, the guitar cushion, and the A-frame. Inquire about these supports at your local guitar dealer.

- Posture is important when playing any musical instrument. Students should keep their backs straight and their shoulders relaxed, and their right arms should rest on the guitar on or just below the elbow.

- Remember to include classic guitar strings in your yearly budget, and to keep an ample supply in stock. You will most likely find that the ④ string, with its thin metal-wound wire, is the first to break, and the thick, nylon ③ string is almost indomitable.

  Strings will usually hold out consistently if you change the entire set twice yearly. A rule of thumb is to change the strings once they have stretched to the point where they no longer need to be tuned. Do not change the strings on more than two or three guitars at one time, since the strings will stretch for a few days and the guitars will be out of commission.

  If time permits during the course, instruct your students in the skill of attaching new strings to a guitar, and allow them to re-string a guitar in small groups.

- Left-handed players will play well on the standard guitar, since both hands are challenged in different ways. They are at an advantage as far as the intricate left-handed work on the fingerboard goes. With minor adjustments to the guitar*, left-handed players can also have the option of holding the guitar the "other way around."

  * To reverse the order of the strings, the grooves in the nut must be adapted to the strings and the bridge must be turned around, so that the higher end is beneath the thicker bass strings. On fine instruments, the bracing system beneath the soundboard, which distributes the sounds evenly, would lose its effectiveness if the guitar were turned around in this manner.

Activities, Student page 7:

- Introduce students to the folk and classic positions shown on student page 7. Provide students with footrests as needed.

- Divide students into groups of two and have them observe each other's playing positions. Until students become comfortable with these positions, this activity should be completed at the beginning of each class session.

2 – CREATING TONES

The best way to hold a guitar is the position that allows you to play with clarity, speed, and expression while remaining comfortable.

Playing Positions

Choose one of the playing positions shown in the illustrations below. A footstool is needed to elevate your leg in the classic position. Then follow these steps:

1. Sit up straight in a chair that offers firm support. Do not slouch.
2. Relax your shoulders.
3. Hold the guitar centered in front of you.
4. Rest the guitar on your elevated leg.

The Folk Position   **The Classic Position**

Teacher Tips, Student page 8:

- The **rest stroke** gives the student an initial stability in the right hand that would otherwise be difficult to achieve.

- The "free stroke" (Spanish "tirando"), which complements the rest stroke, is not introduced in this basic course. This stroke is used for playing chord arpeggios, finger-picking techniques, interval playing, and for a lighter effect in the melody. Teachers who prefer this technique in melody playing may introduce this stroke early on.

- For teachers who prefer using plectrum or steel string guitars, this course is adaptable. The basics that are presented are universal and can be applied to any style of guitar playing.

Activities, Student page 8:

- The knuckle joint of the finger that is playing should hover over the string that is being rested upon. Students should strive for long, slow, full tones rather than short, fast, tinny tones. Students should also try out different angles and analyze the results as well as trying different right hand fingers.

- Explain to students that the tone quality is greatly influenced by the fingertips and fingernails of the right hand. Generally, guitarists play with both fingertip and fingernail. The fingertip provides the strength to pull the string, the fingernail gives the tone brilliance. Fingernails should be smoothly filed and polished to the contour of the fingertips. These should be visible over the fingertips when the palm of the hand is facing the guitarist. Most beginning students will only become aware of the import of the fingernails as the course progresses and they advance in sensitivity.

- Have students practice the *Rest Stroke Exercises* in pairs.

- Have students practice the *Rest Stroke Exercises*, but this time using the **m** and then the **a** finger.

- Have students practice playing long and short tones with single finger rest strokes. Help students develop sensitivity in the right hand by playing loud and soft tones and experimenting with "tone colors." Try the different tone colors: near the bridge (**ponticello**); over the soundhole (**loco**); over the fingerboard (**tasto**).

- If you have a recording of a work by Francisco Tárrega or Andrés Segovia, share it with students.

Interdisciplinary Studies, Student page 8:

- Read the following information about well-known classical guitarists to students:

The Spanish guitarist and composer, **Francisco Tárrega** (1852–1909) developed a systematic technique of playing melodies on the classic guitar that ensures a firm, clear tone with sustain and projection. It was termed "apoyando" ("rest stroke") and has since become standard practice among guitarists worldwide. Tárrega wrote many compositions for solo classical guitar, including *Recuerdos de Aranjuez* and *Capricho Árabe*.

The most famous guitarist to champion the rest stroke was **Andrés Segovia** (1893–1987). A self-taught musician from Spain, Segovia toured the world, performing classical guitar music. He was very influential in bringing audiences to appreciate the guitar as a concert instrument.

The right hand is used to make the strings vibrate and determines if the tone is to be loud or soft, rough or delicate. The fingers of the right hand are named after the first letters of the Spanish words for these fingers:

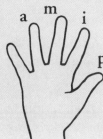

p (pulgar) = **thumb**
i (indios) = **index**
m (medios) = **middle**
a (anular) = **ring**

The Rest Stroke

The rest stroke is a basic plucking motion used to create clear, single tones. Before you play, be sure that your fingernails are short and filed smoothly. Follow these steps to play a rest stroke:

figure A

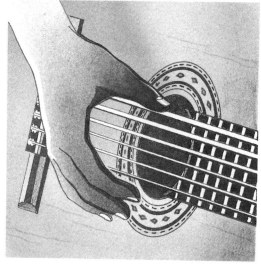

1. Preparation:
   Support your right hand **p** (thumb) on the ⑥ string and arch your right hand and fingers over the strings. To locate the correct playing position, place your **i** (index) fingertip pad on the ① string, and then lift your relaxed **i** finger away from the string from the knuckle joint. (*figure A*)

2. Action:
   Place your **i** finger on the ① string and pull through the string. (*figure B*)

3. Rest:
   Let your **i** finger come to rest on the ② string. (*figure C*) Repeat with the **m** and **a** fingers.

figure B

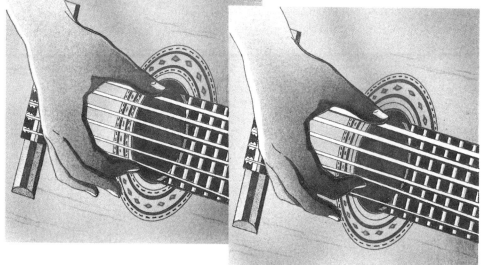

figure C

Rest Stroke Exercises

Play the alternating rest stroke on:
- ☐ the ① string
- ☐ the ② string
- ☐ the ③ string

while playing:
- ☐ quickly
- ☐ slowly
- ☐ alternating between quick and slow

Teacher Tips, Student page 9:

- The **alternating rest stroke** is the basis of smooth playing.

- When repeating a passage using the alternating rest stroke, have students play with the same right hand fingering as used the first time through. This will guarantee a consistency of expression and performance. If the last tone before the repeat is played with the same right hand finger as the first tone, then have students play with this finger again when returning to the repeat.

- Most of the musical examples given in this book are songs, which means that a direct connection with language can be made. The activities provided on student page 9 and below will help students to understand this connection.

Activities, Student page 9:

- To help students understand the advantage of the alternating rest stroke, describe to them the effectiveness of alternating motions, such as car pistons, juggling, etc. Have students use two of their fingers to "walk" around the soundboard of the guitar, and then have them try the alternating rest stroke.

- Have students practice the *Alternating Rest Stroke Exercises* in pairs.

- To develop students' understanding of rhythm, have them try playing common names on their guitars using the alternating rest stroke. The "rhythm" in a name can be connected to the **meters** used in English. Ex.: Mi–chael (long–short), Jen–ni–fer (short–short–long). Have students identify the long-short combinations and accent the appropriate syllables.

- Introduce elements of dynamics by instructing students to express a fellow student's personality when playing his or her name.

- Help students to develop an understanding of a **phrase** as a musical unit through association with language. Have students think of famous sayings, aphorisms or the like and have them "play" these on open strings. Have students experiment with catchy rhythms while playing the phrases, or have them provide an accompaniment while one student plays a phrase.

- Have students try playing a few original aphorisms from Michael Fitzgerald's *Briefly Speaking* (Rainbow's End Books, 1994):

"All art is tribal."
"The poor are the anvils of the rich."
"Dreams are answers as well as questions."
"No noose is good noose."
"The practice of an art form requires courage."
"The main task for trees is to be."

- Ask students to select an aphorism and play it on a single open string for the class, remembering how the words would be accented if spoken. Allow the class to ascertain which aphorism is being played. Have students consider the number of syllables in the phrase and how the syllables are accented.

Just as walking on one leg is difficult, so is using only one finger to play the guitar. While you learn the alternating rest stroke described below, imagine that your **i** (index) and **m** (middle) fingers are miniature legs walking on the strings of the guitar.

figure A

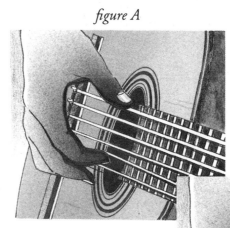

The Alternating Rest Stroke

The alternating rest stroke employs both the **i** and **m** fingers. It is commonly used to play melodies. Follow these steps to play the alternating rest stroke:

1. Preparation:
   Support the right hand **p** (thumb) on the ⑥ string, and arch your right hand and fingers over the strings.

2. Action & Rest:
   Play a rest stroke on the ① string with your **i** finger. *(figure A)* Then, play a rest stroke on the ① string with your **m** finger while moving into position to play another rest stroke with your **i** finger. *(figure B)* Begin the cycle again.

figure B

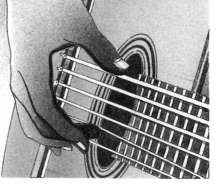

Alternating Rest Stroke Exercises

Play the alternating rest stroke on:
- ☐ the ① string
- ☐ the ② string
- ☐ the ③ string

while playing:
- ☐ quickly
- ☐ slowly
- ☐ alternating between quick and slow strokes

Music and language are both ways to communicate. Words are organized into sentences, and music is organized into phrases. A **phrase** is a musical thought.

"The wood-grain remembers."

This is a saying by poet Michael Fitzgerald. With a partner, think of a few popular sayings, like "Better safe than sorry," and write them down below. Say them out loud, and then play the rhythm of each on one string using the alternating rest stroke. Some tones will be longer, some shorter, some louder, some softer. You have created a musical phrase.

_____

_____

Unit 2 Review
- ☐ guitar playing positions
- ☐ names of the right hand fingers
- ☐ rest stroke
- ☐ alternating rest stroke
- ☐ phrase

Teacher Tips, Student page 10:

• Students may write the counting beneath the notes in the staff in the music throughout the book as needed.

• For more advanced students who can already read music, turn to student page 12 so students can review staff notation and become acquainted with tablature.

Activities, Student page 10:

• Review with students the basics of rhythm and beat presented on student page 10. At the end of the class period, test students on the definitions of **note, time signature, measure, bar lines,** and **beat.**

• Practice clapping the three short musical examples. As students clap, have them say the counting aloud. Ask students to describe how the three time signatures sound different.

• Point out to the students that whole notes cannot occur in a meter smaller than $\frac{4}{4}$.

• Take a walk with the class. Imagine you are all at the mall and each of you is doing her or his own thing. Some are strolling and window shopping, others are hurrying to a particular store. Then you all meet and walk together for a little while. Your feet will fall into step: left-right, left-right. Then you disperse and go your own ways. This image can be transferred onto the guitar when trying to play together in a consistent beat. First everyone plays at his or her own tempo, then everyone meets up and plays together, and then disperses.

• Complete the *March in Time* activity on student page 10 with the class.

• Have students practice playing the alternating rest stroke on an open string in a specific meter with the correct accents in $\frac{2}{4}$, $\frac{3}{4}$, and $\frac{4}{4}$.

• Ask students to practice playing in a specific rhythm (i.e., $\frac{4}{4}$ 𝅗𝅥 ♩ ♩ |) or connect this rhythm to a phrase or name.

• Refer to the musical games on student page 6 and apply these activities to playing on open strings.

• Divide students into groups of two to complete the *Rhythm Review* activity on page 10. This checklist could also be used as a written quiz.

3—READING MUSIC

In music, rhythm is movement. Beat is consistency. Rhythm is expressed in writing with notes. A **note** is a musical symbol which indicates the duration of a sound to be sung or played.

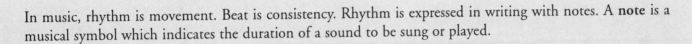

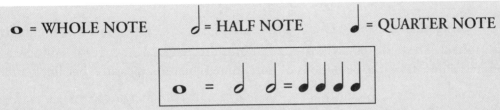

Notes are organized into units called **MEASURES**. Measures are separated by **BAR LINES**. A **DOUBLE BAR LINE** marks the end of the music. A **TIME SIGNATURE**, such as $\frac{2}{4}$, $\frac{4}{4}$, or $\frac{3}{4}$, provides important information about each measure.

In a time signature, the top number indicates the number of **BEATS** per measure. The bottom number indicates the type of note that gets one beat (**4** = quarter note). In $\frac{4}{4}$, a **QUARTER NOTE** gets one beat, a **WHOLE NOTE** gets 4 beats, and a **HALF NOTE** gets 2 beats. Generally, the first beat of each measure is naturally stressed.

In the examples below, counting appears beneath each measure to indicate how many beats each note receives. For half notes and whole notes, ties are drawn to connect the counting numbers to show the duration of the note.

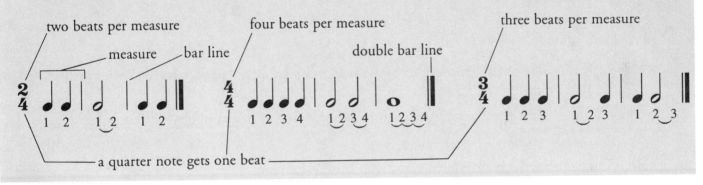

March in Time

With your class, tap your feet on the floor, "Left, Right, Left, Right," as if you were marching. Once you are all tapping at the same speed, count the taps aloud, "1–2, 1–2."

Now, clap each time your left foot taps the floor, so that you are accenting the first beat of this pattern. This is how $\frac{2}{4}$ time feels. Also try clapping and counting in $\frac{3}{4}$ and $\frac{4}{4}$ time.

Rhythm Review

Quiz a partner on the following terms. Define notes in terms of a $\frac{4}{4}$ time signature (for example, "a half note gets two beats in $\frac{4}{4}$ time.") Make a check for each term your partner can define correctly.

☐ note ☐ half note ☐ time signature
☐ whole note ☐ quarter note ☐ measure

Teacher Tip, Student page 11:

• The time signature must be heard by the listener. Too often musicians tend to play with their "eyes" (by concentrating on musical notation) rather than their "ears" (by listening), and disregard the foundation of music making. Throughout this course, students should be encouraged to become increasingly aware of the principles of music accentuation and movement.

Activities, Student page 11:

• Point out to students the difference between how 2 or 4 beats per measure sounds as opposed to 3 beats per measure. Have individual students play on open strings in $\frac{2}{4}$ or $\frac{3}{4}$ time, and have other students ascertain which is being played.

• Play recorded examples of $\frac{2}{4}$, $\frac{4}{4}$, and $\frac{3}{4}$ times for students and have them ascertain which is being played. *Lucy in the Sky with Diamonds* (Lennon/McCartney), for example, changes between $\frac{3}{4}$ and $\frac{4}{4}$.

• Turn on the radio and switch from station to station, asking students to identify the meter and the musical styles of the music being played. Have them first feel the beat and then identify the meter. Ask students to determine whether the beat and the meter are easier to determine in rock music or in classical music.

• Have students complete the exercises on student page 11. When they are finished, practice clapping the exercises as a class. The clapping activity will help students check their answers as well as reinforcing the differences between $\frac{2}{4}$, $\frac{4}{4}$, and $\frac{3}{4}$ time.

Worksheet 2, Student page 11:

• The duplicable Worksheet 2 is provided on page 139. Worksheet 2 provides students with further exercises in rhythm and beat. Distribute the worksheet, and ask students to complete it in class or as a homework assignment. In all ear-training exercises in the worksheets, tap the beat clearly so that students can better understand the different rhythms that are being played.

Quarter Note Quest

Insert bar lines, then play the exercises below on a single string using the alternating rest stroke. Exaggerate the stress on the first beat of each measure to hear the difference between the three exercises. Notice that the three exercises would sound identical without the time signatures.

 Fill in the Blank

Draw <u>one</u> note in each blank to complete the measures below, then play each exercise on a single string.

 Missing Measures

Insert bar lines in the exercises below, then write the counting. Play each exercise on a single string.

Teacher Tips, Student page 12:

- At this point in the course, students will only understand the number "0" in the TAB, meaning open string.

- Students should have already mastered the names of the strings. *Open Strings Only* serves as an orientation to where these tones are found in staff notation and TAB.

Activities, Student page 12:

- Review with students the overview of **staff notation** and **TAB** presented on student page 12.

- Explain the differences between staff notation and TAB in ways that students can easily comprehend.

  Staff notation is like a graph: the higher the **notehead**, the higher the **pitch**; the lower the notehead, the lower the pitch. The direction of the **stem** is irrelevant. The notehead contains information on the duration of the note, or the rhythm.

  TAB (tablature) displays the neck of the guitar in a horizontal position with the lowest sounding string on the bottom. The numbers show behind which fret to stop the string.

- Explain where the treble clef gets the name G-clef. Draw the following example on the board.

- Write out the noteheads of the open strings in random order on the board. Have students identify and play each of these notes.

- Read the following history of tablature to students:

  Until the mid-18th century, guitarists used tablature (TAB) systems exclusively to write down and read music. After that time, they began to use the more universal staff notation system. TAB is used today by folk and rock guitarists, often in combination with staff notation.

- Complete the *Open Strings Only* exercise with students in class.

Worksheet 3, Student page 12:

- The duplicable Worksheet 3 is provided on page 140. Worksheet 3 reinforces students' understanding of writing and reading staff notation and TAB.

In guitar music, pitch is expressed in writing using three different kinds of notation: staff notation, tablature (TAB), and chord charts. Staff notation and tablature (TAB) are often combined, and will be introduced here together. Chord charts will be introduced on page 21.

STAFF NOTATION provides information on the highness or lowness of the pitches to be sung or played. The group of 5 lines is called a **STAFF**. The higher a note falls on the staff, the higher the pitch. The lower a note falls on the staff, the lower the pitch. **LEDGER LINES** are short lines that represent a continuation of the staff. They are used to indicate notes that fall above or below the staff.

A **CLEF** is a symbol which indicates the position of pitches on the staff. A **TREBLE CLEF** (𝄞), for example, shows that the second line from the bottom of the staff is the pitch G. The other pitches on the staff can be determined by knowing this pitch.

TABLATURE (TAB) provides information on where to play the pitches on the guitar itself. The six lines of the TAB represent the six strings of the guitar. The top line is the highest-sounding string. Numbers written on the lines signify the fret behind which your left hand should be pressing.

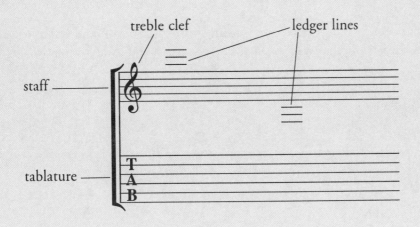

 ## Open Strings Only

In the exercise below, first read the staff notation, playing each open string as indicated by the notes on the staff. Say each note aloud as you play. Then, read the tablature. The 0 indicates that you should play an open string (without any left hand fingers pressing down).

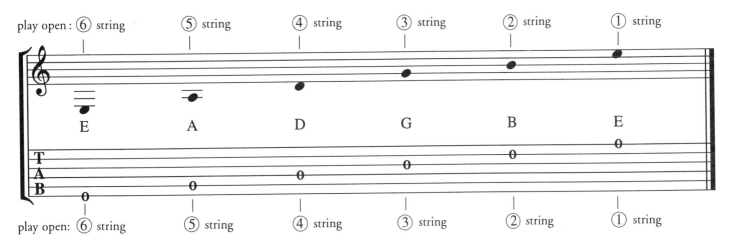

Teacher Tip, Student page 13:

• Although the **i** and **m** fingers will be used primarily, introduce the **a** (ring) finger and use it in combinations of the alternating rest stroke. Exercising the **a** finger will help the **i** and **m** fingers become more independent.

Activities, Student page 13:

• Have students write in the TAB for *Three String Studies.* Then have some students play while others clap the rhythm. Switch roles and repeat.

• To help students feel the long dotted half note value, have half of the class count or clap quarter notes while the other half of the class plays exercise #3 of *Three String Studies.* Students should place the emphasis in the correct place in the meter.

• Introduce the musical symbol meaning **accent** (>) to students. Have them draw in accents above or below the noteheads in *Three String Studies* to remind them to place an emphasis on the first beat of each measure.

• Ask students to structure words and phrases into rhythms using half notes and quarter notes. This will help reinforce these note values, as well as the difference between $\frac{3}{4}$ and $\frac{4}{4}$ time.

Staff notation may be used to indicate not only the highness or lowness of pitches, but also, the rhythm in which pitches should be sung or played.

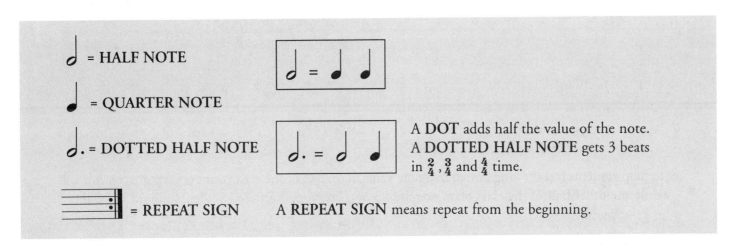

♩ = HALF NOTE

♩ = QUARTER NOTE

♩. = DOTTED HALF NOTE   A **DOT** adds half the value of the note. A **DOTTED HALF NOTE** gets 3 beats in $\frac{2}{4}$, $\frac{3}{4}$ and $\frac{4}{4}$ time.

= REPEAT SIGN   A **REPEAT SIGN** means repeat from the beginning.

Three String Studies

In the exercises below, fill in the TAB. Exercise 1 has been completed for you. (Notice the rhythm is not shown in the TAB notation.) Then, play each exercise using the alternating rest stroke. The **i** and **m** fingerings are marked. Use the counting below each line of music to help you play accurately.

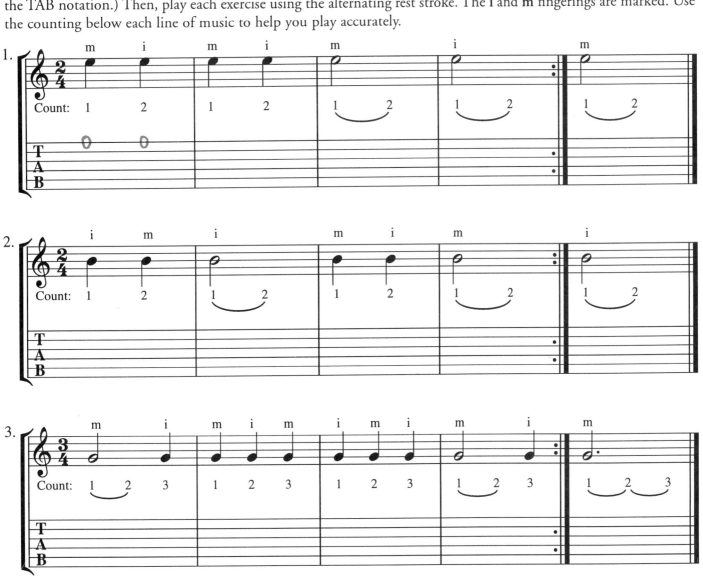

WG108T

Teacher Tips, Student page 14:

- It is important that students understand when traversing the strings with the right hand that they must move the entire forearm from the elbow. This guarantees a consistency of tone production that could not be achieved if the fingers stretched and bent to reach the strings to be played.

- *Across the Strings* can be referred to throughout the course since these exercises consolidate a sensitive right hand touch.

- As students play *Across the Strings*, remind them to use the alternating rest stroke, and to pay attention to where the natural accent falls in each measure.

Activities, Student page 14:

- Review the instructions for *Across the Strings* and the illustration provided on student page 14. Demonstrate the correct motion for students.

- Have students insert the bar lines, write in the names of the notes, and fill in the TAB for *Across the Strings* before playing. Then rehearse each exercise with students.

- Divide the class into small groups. Have group members analyze the playing technique of their classmates. Have students concentrate on the alternating rest stroke and moving the right arm correctly when changing strings.

Units 2 & 3 Quiz, Student page 14:

- The duplicable Units 2 & 3 Quiz is provided on page 146. The quiz asks students to write short compositions of their own in staff and TAB, and to perform their compositions for the class. The quiz can be completed as a take-home assignment or an in-class quiz. Asking students to perform their compositions for the class, while time-consuming, will require students to bring together all of the elements of guitar playing and music reading and writing that they have learned thus far, and is a useful means of testing students' comprehension.

Across the Strings

When moving between higher and lower strings with your right hand, the movement should be from your elbow, rather than from stretching and closing your fingers. This will create consistent tone production.

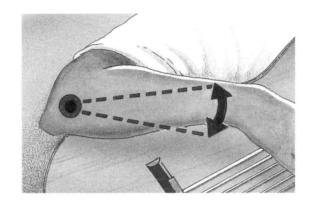

On the open string exercises below, use the right arm technique depicted above to switch strings as you play. Insert bar lines, write the names of the notes below the staff, and fill in the TAB. Exercise 1 has been completed for you. Then, play each exercise using the alternating rest stroke.

1.
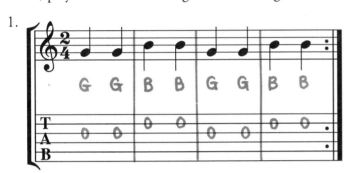

2.

3.

4.

5.

6.

Unit 3 Review

☐ note	☐ measure	☐ beat	☐ clef	☐ dotted half note
☐ whole note	☐ bar line	☐ staff notation	☐ treble clef	☐ repeat sign
☐ half note	☐ double bar line	☐ staff	☐ tablature (TAB)	
☐ quarter note	☐ time signature	☐ ledger lines	☐ dot	

Teacher Tips, Student page 15:

- VII Position has been chosen as a starting point for students because the distance between the frets is small, which allows students to comfortably reach four frets with all four fingers without having to stretch too much. Once students feel comfortable with VII Position, repeat *The Left Hand* exercise in I Position or other positions.

- Look for a consistent arch in the left hand fingers, with the fingertips pressing down on the strings.

- Remind students that the numbers in the TAB are the *fret numbers*, not the *left hand finger numbers*. Although the distinction is not apparent in I Position, students will be able to adjust more easily to playing in higher positions if they understand this concept.

- In order to keep track of school guitars, it is important to number or name all of the guitars, and assign to each a hard-shell case. Maintain a strict sign-out policy. Keep a sign-out book for guitars in the classroom. Draw up a contract for students and/or parents which clearly states that guitars are to be transported in their hard-shell cases and that the student who signs out the guitar is the sole person responsible for the care of that instrument until it is returned to the classroom. Nurture in students a sense of respect and responsibility for the guitar as a finely-crafted instrument.

- A special area should be created in the classroom where each guitar can be safely stored outside its case for easy student access. Consult with your school and your local music instrument dealer about designing and creating this area. For example, a row of vertical, felt- or carpet-lined compartments could be built for storing the guitars upright with the heads leaning on the back wall. Alternatively, a system of padded supports could be constructed to hold the guitars at the point where the neck widens into the head, allowing the guitars to hang freely in a vertical position.

- Establishing a guitar resource library for the classroom of printed and recorded guitar music and reference books will be an ongoing project. Concentrate on obtaining music that will benefit the majority of your students for the longest period of time. The music should represent a wide variety of musical styles and types of guitars. Refer to student pages 2–3 and to Worksheet 1: A Brief History of the Guitar (page 138) for suggestions of styles and artists. Rather than purchasing current hits for your library, encourage students to bring in their own CDs or tapes to share with the class. Organize the printed music, reference books, and CDs or tapes so that students can make use of the guitar resource library at designated times. Your printed music collection can be further supplemented by arrangements which you prepare yourself for classroom use.

Activities, Student page 15:

- Review the instructions for playing with the left hand provided on student page 15. Students may be confused about where to place their fingers in relationship to the frets. The finger should fall as close to the fret as possible, on the left side of the fret (the side closer to the nut). Complete the exercise together with the class.

- Ask students to notice how the distance between the frets in the upper positions differs from the distance between the frets in the lower positions.

- Divide the class into small groups, and have students carefully observe one another's hand positions.

- Play the "guessing game" on a single string. Have one student play a tone, and ask others to find this tone on their own guitars by experimenting, and not by looking at the other student's hand position.

- Ask students to identify, by listening and experimenting, where the open string pitches can be found on other strings using the left hand.

4 – Changing Pitch

The left hand is used to change the pitch of the strings you are playing. To change the pitch, press the fingertip(s) directly behind the indicated fret(s), which are the metal bars across the fingerboard. Pressing the string changes the length of the string, thus changing its pitch. The fingers of the left hand are numbered:

1 = index
2 = middle
3 = ring
4 = small

The Left Hand

Follow these steps to position your left hand:

1. Preparation:

   With the guitar in playing position (see page 7), let your left arm hang loosely from the shoulder. Then, swing your left hand up to the neck of the guitar and grasp it lightly.

2. Position:

   On the ① string, slide your 1 (index) finger directly behind (to the left of) the 7th fret. Place your 2 (middle) finger similarly behind the 8th fret, leaving the 1 finger in place. Then, allow your 3 and 4 fingers to fall behind the 9th and 10th frets. Place your thumb flat against the back of the neck of the guitar in a position opposite the 1 and 2 fingers.

3. Press:

   Press your fingertips on the strings. When you remove your hand from the strings, the indentations in your fingers show the parts of your fingertips which should always press the strings.

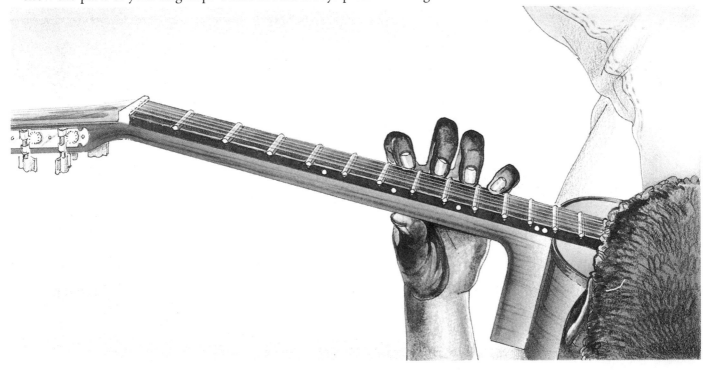

Teacher Tips, Student page 16:

- Remind students that, in order to maintain correct placement, they should keep the 1 finger on the string as much as possible. The 2 finger should also be kept on the string while playing the 3 finger note, and the 2 and 3 fingers should be kept on the string when the 4 finger is played.

- *Basic Notes in I Position* is the most important reference chart in the student book. Students may refer to this chart at any time if they are searching for how to play a particular note.

- Students without prior musical training will prefer TAB because it is practical in its application and offers a shortcut to music-making. Beginning with the second song, *Down in the Valley*, songs in this book are generally given in staff notation with blank TAB lines below for students to fill in. These can be given as homework assignments with an honor code of not copying from others, or can be completed independently in class. The purpose is to familiarize students with the notes and their names in staff notation. Let students know the purpose of TAB, and that they will be tested on their ability to fill in TAB. Later on in the book, music will be presented solely in staff notation.

- Plan to begin each practice session with right and left hand exercises in I and VII Position until students become comfortable with both high and low positions. Although the majority of the songs in the method are in I or II Position, teaching students to play in higher positions will familiarize them with the fingerboard. Have students play each tone four times in order to allow time for correction.

- Explain that the distance between two adjacent frets is a **half step**, and that the distance between every other fret is a **whole step** (student page 26). Have students identify pairs of notes in *Basic Notes in I Position* which are a half step apart by circling those pairs of notes in their books.

Activities, Student page 16:

- Explain to students that **positions** on the guitar are defined by the fret that the left hand first finger is placed behind. Positions are indicated with Roman numerals to differentiate them from other fingerings. A position generally includes a range of four frets, with each finger of the left hand responsible for one fret.

- Have students observe the steps in preparation for left hand playing. Have students try the steps on different strings and in different positions to prepare them for the *Nimble Fingers* exercise.

- Divide the class into two groups. Complete the *Nimble Fingers* exercise. Then complete the exercise again, but this time have one group begin playing with the 4 finger while the other group begins with the 1 finger in the reverse direction. As a preparation for hearing consonances and dissonances (student page 45) have students listen for notes which sound pleasant together, and those that do not.

- Complete the *Nimble Fingers* exercise but have students experiment with different rhythms and meters.

- Complete the *Nimble Fingers* exercise using rhythmic phrases connected with words.

- Review *Basic Notes in I Position* with students. Explain to students that they can refer to this chart in the future for finding notes.

The fingerboard of the guitar is divided into positions. The position is named for the fret that the 1 (index) finger plays. In the instructions on page 15, the 1 finger was placed behind the 7th fret. This is 7th or VII Position.

 Nimble Fingers

Place your left hand in VII Position as described on page 15. Then, using the alternating rest stroke, play the 4 finger note four times using even strokes, then the 3 finger note, then the 2 finger note, and then the 1 finger note. Your fingers should lift off of the fingerboard as you play each successive note of this exercise.

Now, play the 1 finger note, and then place the 2 finger down and play the note (keeping the 1 finger on the string as well). Then do the same with the 3 finger, and the 4 finger. Experiment with performing the same exercise in other positions and on other strings. Notice that the stretch between your fingers is wider on the lower frets.

 Basic Notes in I Position

Generally, the music in this book will be given in staff notation. You will fill in the TAB. The basic notes played in 1st or I Position, are shown below to serve as a reference for you as you play the songs in the rest of the book. The numbers on the lines indicate the frets behind which you should press your left hand fingers. Practice these notes to become familiar with them.

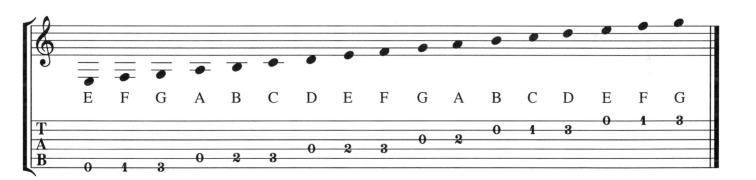

Teacher Tips, Student page 17:

• The *Both Hands* exercises will help prepare students for playing the first melodies and scales. Have students concentrate on a smooth transition between notes. They can create a smooth transition by preparing the left hand fingers by leaving them on the notes.

• Watch that students place their left hand fingers down at the same time as they play with the right hand.

Warm-up, Student page 17:

• Have students complete the *Nimble Fingers* exercise on student page 16.

• Rehearse the *Basic Notes in I Position*.

Activities, Student page 17:

• Have students complete the *Both Hands* exercises. Each exercise trains a particular finger or fingers.

Exercises 1 & 2: Train the 2 finger, which is the strongest and most confident finger of the left hand. The other left hand fingers should remain relaxed. Be sure that students place the finger on its fingertip directly behind the fret and lift it off directly to ensure a clear tone.

Exercise 3: Train the 3 finger. Place the 1 and 2 fingers behind the 1st and 2nd frets on the string together while moving the 3 finger to develop a solid technique.

Exercises 4 & 5: Prepare the 1 finger by leaving it on the string while playing the 3 finger. Do this by placing the 1 and 2 fingers on the string together with the 3 finger.

Exercise 6: Practice the same movement learned in exercises 4 and 5 on another string.

Exercises 7 & 8: Prepare the tones using the principles of preparation described above. These exercises traverse two strings.

• As students play each exercise, have them observe the time signature and emphasize the first beat in each measure.

BLUES IN A

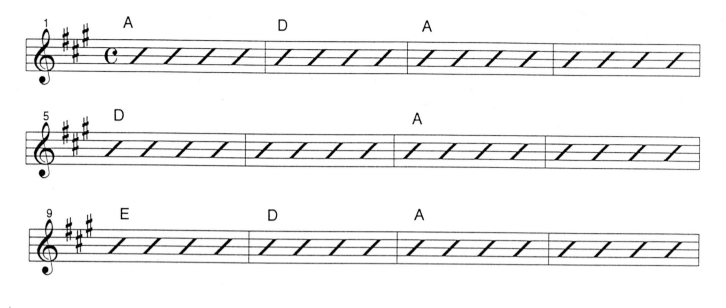

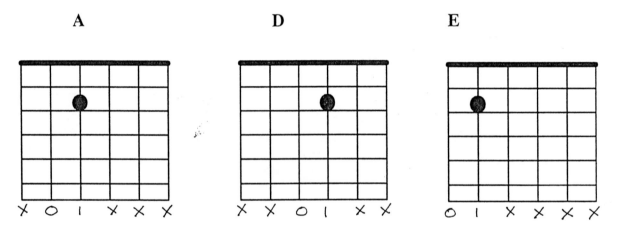

STRUM WITH A PICK USING A STRAIGHT 8THS FEEL (ROCK/BLUES) **OR A** SWING FEEL (BLUES/SHUFFLE).

STRUM ONLY THE STRINGS INDICATED WITH AN "O" OR A FINGER NUMBER (1).

IMPROVING

TO IMPROVISE OVER THE 12-BAR BLUES IN A, START BY IDENTIFYING THE ROOT NOTE FRET IN THE KEY OF A. THIS IS THE FRET WHERE "A" IS LOCATED ON THE 6TH AND 1ST STRINGS (FIFTH FRET). EVERY NOTE AT THIS FRET IS IN THE A MINOR PENTATONIC SCALE.

BEGIN BY USING THESE FOUR NOTES, DIAGRAMMED BELOW.
START PLAYING ON THE HIGHEST NOTE (1ST STRING/8TH FRET)

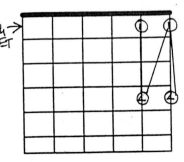

WORK YOUR WAY DOWN THROUGH THE TOP 4 NOTES .
OF THE SCALE
COME UP WITH PATTERNS THAT SOUND GOOD TO YOU.

Both Hands

In the exercises below, insert bar lines, write the names of the notes, and fill in the TAB. Exercise 1 has been completed for you. Then, play all eight exercises using the alternating rest stroke.

1.
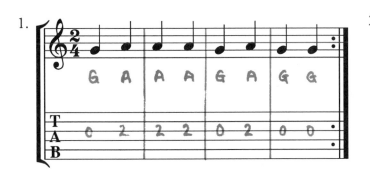

2.

3.

4.

5.

6.

7.

8.

Teacher Tips, Student page 18:

• Counting is provided in the student edition, but have students apply the counting system that you prefer.

• Be sure that students subdivide the quarter notes when writing in the counting.

• Exercises 3, 5, and 6 of *Eighth Note Exercises on Open Strings* prepare students for the first song students will learn, *Hush, Little Baby* on student page 19.

Exercise 3 is the rhythm of the first two measures of the song on a single open string.

Exercise 5 is the same rhythm as exercise 3, only across the strings. Watch out for the jump from the ③ to the ① string. Remind students to move the right forearm.

Exercise 6 is similar to the rhythm, across the strings, of the third and fourth measures of *Hush, Little Baby.*

• Watch that students use good posture and the correct right and left hand playing positions.

Activities, Student page 18:

• Have students fill in the TAB and the counting for *Eighth Note Exercises on Open Strings* before they play.

• Divide the class into three sections. Have one group clap quarter notes, another group clap or tap eighth notes, and the third group play the *Eighth Note Exercises on Open Strings.*

• Have students create new two-measure exercises in $\frac{4}{4}$ time as a homework assignment or in class with a partner.

• Complete the Unit 4 Review checklist with students.

Worksheet 4, Student page 18:

• The duplicable Worksheet 4 is provided on page 141. Worksheet 4 asks students to compose short, two-tone melodies in staff notation. Students are then asked to listen to other students play their compositions, to notate the rhythms played, and to recognize the pattern of tones played.

Unit 4 Quiz, Student page 18:

• The duplicable Unit 4 Quiz is provided on page 147. The Unit 4 Quiz tests students on left hand finger numbers, eighth note rhythms, and the basic notes in I Position.

♪ = EIGHTH NOTE   An EIGHTH NOTE gets ¹/₂ beat in $\frac{2}{4}$, $\frac{3}{4}$, and $\frac{4}{4}$ time.

Eighth Note Exercises on Open Strings

In the exercises below, fill in the TAB and write the counting for each measure. Exercise 1 has been completed for you. As you play each exercise, count eighth notes evenly out loud: "1 & 2 & 3 & 4 &."

1.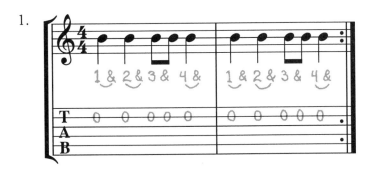

2.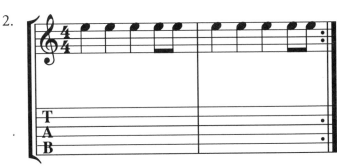

3.

4.

5.

6.

Unit 4 Review

☐ left hand finger numbers
☐ using the left hand
☐ eighth notes

☐ names of the left hand positions
☐ playing basic notes in I Position

Teacher Tips, Student page 19:

- The three building blocks of guitar ensemble music — melody, chords, and bass tones — are introduced in Unit 5. Starting on student page 28, tips for playing the melody, chords, and bass lines are clearly displayed before most songs.

- The lyrics are included here and in other songs to establish a closer connection between language and music. In the realm of pure instrumental music, words can often make phrases easier to understand. Ludwig van Beethoven once said that if a musical phrase is difficult to understand, place words beneath it. (Anton Schindler, *Beethoven Biographie,* p.588)

- While students play the song, accompany them with chords or bass tones, as described on student pages 21 and 23. By performing the song with a chord or bass tone accompaniment, students will already be familiar with how the accompaniment lines should sound when they learn them.

Warm-up, Student page 19:

- Have students play *Eighth Note Exercises on Open Strings,* on student page 18, together.

Activities, Student page 19:

- Students can now apply the skills they have learned to play songs. Before they play, students should master the five tones used in the song (G, C, D, E, F) and answer the questions provided.

- Ask students how many different rhythmic values appear in *Hush, Little Baby*.

- Have students observe that the melody tones in the first line (measures 1–4) are identical to those in the second line (measures 5–8). However, the rhythm is slightly altered to fit the syllables of the lyrics.

- Have some students sing the song while others play the melody.

5 – FIRST SONGS

Now you know the fundamentals of reading music and playing the guitar. Let's put these skills to work by learning the three building blocks of guitar music: melody, chords, and bass lines. First, we will become familiar with two well-known melodies — *Hush, Little Baby* and *Down in the Valley*.

 Hush, Little Baby

Hush, Little Baby uses the following tones:

Before you play the song, answer these questions:

1. What is the time signature?
2. What is the highest note? What is the lowest note?
3. What is the shortest note? What is the longest note?
4. How many different notes are there?

Once you can answer all of the questions, play *Hush, Little Baby*.

Hush, Little Baby

Southern Lullaby

Teacher Tips, Student page 20:

• While students play *Down in the Valley*, accompany them with chords or bass tones, as described on student pages 21 and 23. By hearing the song played with a chord or bass tone accompaniment, students will already be familiar with how the accompaniment lines should sound when they learn them.

• Students should be reminded to count 6 beats silently during the tied notes before continuing, even though the sound may have died out. When a chord strum or bass line is added, the beats will not sound like beats of rest.

Warm-up, Student page 20:

• Review the meaning of $\frac{3}{4}$ time with students (3 beats per measure, each beat is a quarter note). Have students identify how a time signature affects a song.

• Have students play the right column of exercises in *Both Hands* on student page 17 to review how to play in $\frac{3}{4}$ time.

Activities, Student page 20:

• One more tone is included in *Down in the Valley* than in *Hush, Little Baby*. Have students identify the tone, and have them use *Basic Notes in I Position* on student page 16 to find and name it.

• Explain to students that ties are used to extend a note longer than the duration of a measure. Review with students the definition of **tie** provided on student page 20. In *Down in the Valley*, notes are extended to 6 beats instead of 3.

• Have some students sing the song while others play the melody.

Interdisciplinary Studies, Student page 20:

• Read the following passage on the origin of *Down in the Valley* to students:

Down in the Valley as we know it was first sung by the people of the Appalachian Mountains in Kentucky in the 19th century. The song became well-known throughout early America, and was passed down from generation to generation. Some of North America's oldest folk songs come from the Appalachian Mountains.

A **TIE** is a curved line that connects two notes of the same pitch to make one, longer note value.

Count: 1   2   3   1   2   3

 Down in the Valley

Fill in the TAB to this song, as you have done on previous exercises. Then, perform the *Down in the Valley* melody, remembering that ¾ has a different character than 4/4. Before you begin playing, identify the highest and lowest notes, and the longest and shortest notes.

Down in the Valley

Kentucky Mountain Song

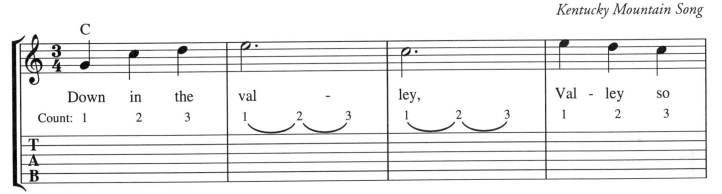

Down   in   the   val   -   ley,   Val - ley so

Count: 1   2   3   1   2   3   1   2   3   1   2   3

low._____   _____   Hang your head   o   -

       1   2   3   1   2   3

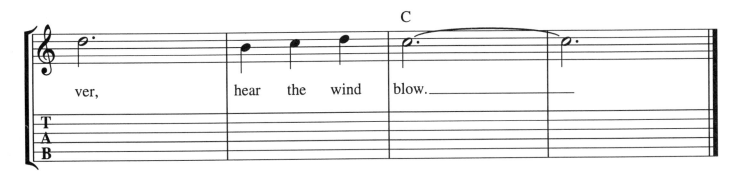

ver,   hear   the   wind   blow._____   _____

WG108T

Teacher Tips, Student page 21:

- While students are learning to strum chords, watch that students' right forearms and wrists are relaxed when strumming the strings with the fingers or the thumb.

- Students should strive to simultaneously lift the fingers of the left hand off the strings and then place them on the strings to play the next chord. They should avoid letting fingers crawl finger by finger from one chord to the next.

- Remind students to press the strings with the fingertips of the left hand. This is important with the simplified C Major chord, because the open ① string has to be heard.

- Help students recognize where a chord changes by counting through a piece and clapping at the chord change. If students are having difficulty, have them listen for a key word in the lyrics, or for a change in the melody.

Warm-up, Student page 21:

- Have students play *Hush, Little Baby* and *Down in the Valley* (student pages 19 and 20) to prepare them for learning the chord accompaniment for each piece.

Activities, Student page 21:

- Review the instructions for playing chords with students.

- Have students play the *First Chords* exercises together. Then have students use the chord symbols provided in *Hush, Little Baby* (student page 19) and *Down in the Valley* (student page 20) to play the chord progressions for each piece.

- Divide the class into two groups. Have one group play *Hush, Little Baby* (student page 19) while the other group plays the chords as marked by the chord symbols above the music. Switch roles and repeat. Once students have mastered *Hush, Little Baby*, have them do the same activity with *Down in the Valley* (student page 20).

- Have students accompany *Hush, Little Baby* (student page 20) and *Down in the Valley* (student page 21) "by ear." This activity can be done before or after students have become familiar with playing the chord progressions as provided in the music. Establish a steady beat in the right hand, with an accent on the first beat of each measure.

- Select other songs with the I–V7 (C–G7) chords and have students accompany you by ear.

The second building block in guitar music is chords. Chords are often represented in written guitar music by chord charts, a form of notation.

A **CHORD** is three or more tones played as a unit. The tones can be played at the same time or played one after the other. Every chord has a name (such as "C" or "G7") which is determined by the notes in the chord. **STRUM** chords by letting your fingernails or your thumb glide down over the strings.

CHORD CHARTS provide information on where to play chords on the guitar. In *First Chords*, the vertical lines are the strings, running from lowest to highest, and the horizontal lines are frets. The double line on the top represents the nut. A black dot shows where the finger should be pressing. A number inside the dot indicates which left hand finger should be used. The number "0" above a string indicates that the string should be played open, with no frets pressed down. If there is no number or black dot indicated for a string, the string should not be played.

 First Chords

Two simple chords that are played on the top three strings of the guitar are C and G7. Play the chords by strumming the top three strings from the ③ string to the ① string.

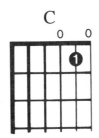   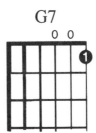

After you are comfortable with the basic strumming technique, play the exercise below. Strive to change from the C chord to the G7 chord without missing a beat.

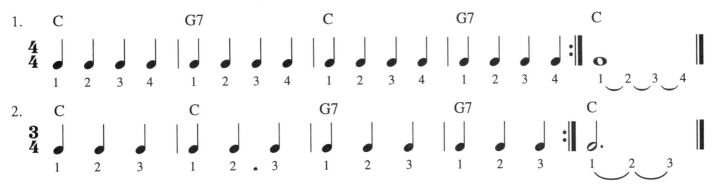

 Accompaniment Activity

Use the C and G7 chords to accompany the melodies on *Hush, Little Baby* (page 19) and *Down in the Valley* (page 20). Above the staff notation, the C or G7 indicates which chord should be played during each measure. Strum one chord per beat just as you did in *First Chords*. Some students in your class can play the melody while others play the chords, or you can play the chords by yourself and sing along. End the accompaniment by letting the last chord ring out.

Teacher Tips, Student page 22:

- The low bass strings are most commonly played with the thumb (**p**). The thumb stroke produces its own characteristic sound. The early introduction into the thumb playing technique paves the way for gratifying ensemble playing throughout this course. It also prepares students for advanced solo playing, in which the thumb works together with the fingers.

- While students are learning to play bass tones, watch that students keep their right hand fingers arched over the strings.

- The thumb plays with a circular "free stroke" (Spanish: "tirando"). This allows for a rapid recovery to prepare for the next bass tone.

- For students who are interested in learning to play the bass, an electric bass guitar (or upright double bass) can be provided for playing bass line accompaniments. The four strings of both instruments are tuned to the same tones as the four lower strings of the guitar, but an octave lower.

Warm-up, Student page 22:

- Have students play the *First Chords* exercises on student page 21.

Activities, Student page 22:

- Review the instructions for playing bass tones with the thumb with students. Demonstrate the motion for students, and have them play a repeated tone with you.

- Have students fill in the TAB and write the names of the notes below the staff on *Open Bass Strings*. Have students refer to *Open Strings Only* on student page 12 to remind them of how to play these bass strings. Then have students complete the exercises as a group.

The third building block of guitar music is bass tones, which emphasize important tones in the chords, and provide a solid foundation for the melody. Bass tones are played on the ⑥, ⑤, and ④ strings.

Playing Bass Tones with the Thumb

In order to play bass tones, or low tones, you need to play the ⑥, ⑤, and ④ strings. For now, use the following technique when playing these strings as part of a bass line.

1. Preparation:
   Place your **i**, **m**, and **a** fingers on the ③, ② , and ① strings respectively. Arch the back of your hand over the strings and rest your thumb on the ⑥ string.

2. Action:
   Strike the open ⑥ string with your thumb using clockwise motions. Do not rest your thumb on the next higher string. *(See figure at right.)*

Open Bass Strings

Fill in the TAB, and write the names of the notes below the staff. Then, play the exercises using your thumb. Refer to *Open Strings Only* (page 12) to locate these low notes.

1.

2.

3.

4.

5.

6.

Teacher Tip, Student page 23:

• Students will often gravitate towards either playing melodies, strumming chords, or playing bass tones. Each is a valid form of individual expression and should be cultivated and encouraged. However, by requiring students to learn all three parts of a musical selection, they will become more sensitive to how the whole fits together and how they are contributing to it.

Warm-up, Student page 23:

• Have students review the correct playing positions for chords and bass tones. Have them play the *Open Bass Strings* exercises (student page 22) together.

• Divide the class into two groups, and have one group play the melody of *Hush, Little Baby* (student page 19) while the other group performs the chords. Switch roles and repeat. Repeat the activity with *Down in the Valley* (student page 20).

Activities, Student page 23:

• Have students fill in the TAB for the *All Thumbs* exercises. Then have them play the exercises together.

• For students who are having difficulty crossing strings while playing with their thumbs, remind them to anchor their **i**, **m**, and **a** fingers on the top three strings so that the hand is stabilized.

• Review with students the instructions for *Bass Tone Accompaniment*. Have students play the bass tones in the exercise to prepare for accompanying *Hush, Little Baby* and *Down in the Valley* (student pages 19 and 20).

• Have students play the bass tones rather than the chords this time in *Hush, Little Baby* and *Down in the Valley* (student pages 19 and 20). Have students play once each measure on the first beat. Then divide the class into two groups, and have one group play the melody for each song while the other group plays the bass tones. Switch roles and repeat.

• For more advanced students, have them try playing rhythms in the bass tones.

• Once students are comfortable with playing the melody, chords, and bass tones, divide the class into groups and have them practice various combinations with both songs.

• The exercise below for bass playing with chords is for students who advance quickly and are looking for further challenges. This exercise can be used to accompany *Hush, Little Baby* (student page 19). Demonstrate the exercise for students to show how bass and chord playing can be combined. Play the bass tone with the thumb, and strum the chord tones with a downstroke with the **m** finger.

Bass/chord exercise:

All Thumbs

Write in the TAB, then play the exercises below using your thumb. Refer to *Basic Notes in I Position* (page 16) to locate the left hand fingerings for these low notes.

1.
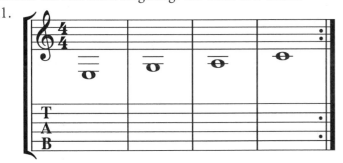

2.

3.
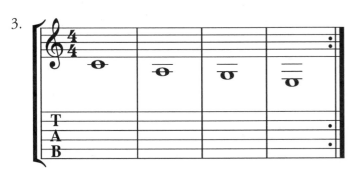

4.

5.
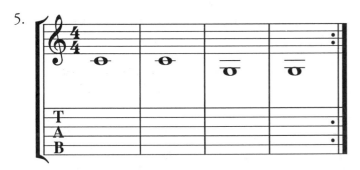

6.

> A bass tone accompaniment on a song reinforces the root of the chord indicated in the music. The root of a chord is the note with the same name as that of the chord. For example, the root of the C Major chord is C.

Bass Tone Accompaniment

Return to *Hush, Little Baby* (page 19). While some students play the melody and some play the chords, create a bass line by adding the bass tone C on the first beat of each measure where a C chord is designated. In the same manner, add a bass tone G where a G7 chord is indicated. Listen to the effect. The first line of the bass tone accompaniment is shown below.

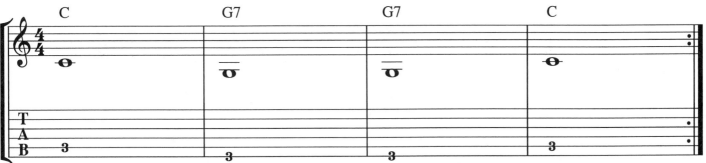

Teacher Tip, Student page 24:

• Once plucked, guitar strings continue to vibrate with rapidly decreasing amplitude until dampened. This applies also to "sympathetic vibrations," which are vibrations on open strings caused by octaves or overtones. Often, a string must be dampened so that its vibrations do not interfere with the clear sound of a newly-played string, even though a rest may not be specified. The vibrations caused by tones on the higher strings are short-lived and rarely pose a problem. However, unwanted bass tones vibrate longer. To avoid a muddled sound in the bass line, dampen the vibrating open bass string lightly with the thumb directly before playing the next bass tone.

Activities, Student page 24:

• Review the definition of **rest** provided on student page 24. Define a rest as an absence of sound.

• Explain to students that a rest must be "played" on the guitar by dampening the vibrating string. Actively playing the rest will result in a better defined sense of the rhythmic value of the rest, rather than just letting the tone play on through the rest to the next tone.

• Explain to students that rests are used to define phrases, to emphasize notes, to let other parts be heard more clearly, and to create tension or relaxation, suspense or resolution.

• Have students play *A Moment of Silence* together. Confirm that students use the correct fingers to dampen the strings.

• Make a connection between the use of rests in music and pauses or rests in spoken language. Ask students how rests are effectively used in a sentence. Have students create examples of how a speaker may use rests. Have them also try inserting rests into simple phrases, such as the aphorisms discussed on student page 9.

• Have students practice drawing the musical symbols for rests on blank staffs or on the board. Have them make a connection between the rests and their counterparts in notes.

A **REST** is a symbol representing the duration of a silence in music. For each note value there is a corresponding rest value.

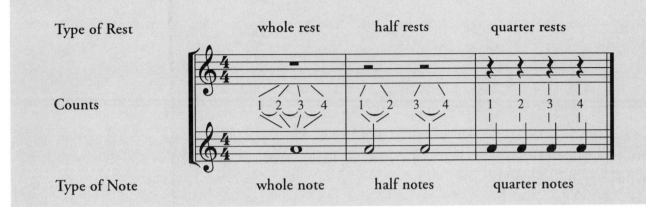

Type of Rest	whole rest	half rests	quarter rests

To perform a rest on the guitar, you must stop the vibration of the strings. To do this, place the fingertip(s) or the thumb of the right hand on the vibrating string(s).

A Moment of Silence

In exercises 1–4 below, write the counting under all notes and rests. Exercise 1 has been completed for you. Then, play the exercises, carefully observing the **i** and **m** indications above the staff. When (**i**) or (**m**) appears, use the indicated finger to dampen the string just played. Leave the finger on the string for the duration of the rest.

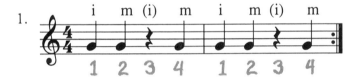

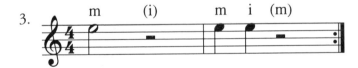

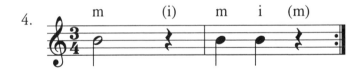

In exercises 5–6, play the notes and rests using your thumb (**p**). Notice that a whole rest is used to indicate a measure rest in $\frac{3}{4}$ time.

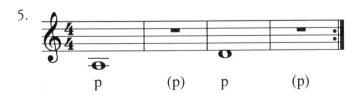

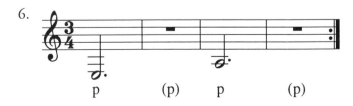

Activities, Student page 25:

- Review the definitions of **eighth note** and **dotted quarter note** provided on student page 25 with students.

- Have students practice clapping the dotted quarter note against eighth notes in preparation for the *Count the Dots* exercise.

- Have students fill in the TAB and write the counting for the top line of *Count the Dots*. Then divide the class into two groups. Have one group play the melody while the other group claps the second line. Switch roles and repeat.

- Ask students to associate the dotted quarter note and eighth note rhythms they have learned with proper names, such as names of cities. Once students have associated rhythms with a few cities, have them clap, tap, or play the rhythm while saying the name.

Examples:

- Divide the class into four groups, and assign each group a rhythm above. Combine these four rhythmic patterns so that all four groups are playing or clapping simultaneously. Variations: a) Assign each group a percussive sound to play in order to distinguish between the rhythmic patterns. b) Assign each group a chord tone so that students can experience the harmonic effect of different notes played together.

- Have students complete the Unit 5 Review checklist in pairs.

Unit 5 Quiz, Student page 25:

- The duplicable Unit 5 Quiz is provided on page 148. The Unit 5 Quiz tests students on rests, ties, and how to analyze a song before playing.

♪ = EIGHTH NOTE

♩. = DOTTED QUARTER NOTE

An eighth note gets a ½ beat in $\frac{2}{4}$, $\frac{3}{4}$, and $\frac{4}{4}$ time.

A DOTTED QUARTER NOTE gets 1½ beats in $\frac{2}{4}$, $\frac{3}{4}$, and $\frac{4}{4}$ time.

 Count the Dots

Write the counting for the exercises below. Then, play each exercise with a partner or with your class.

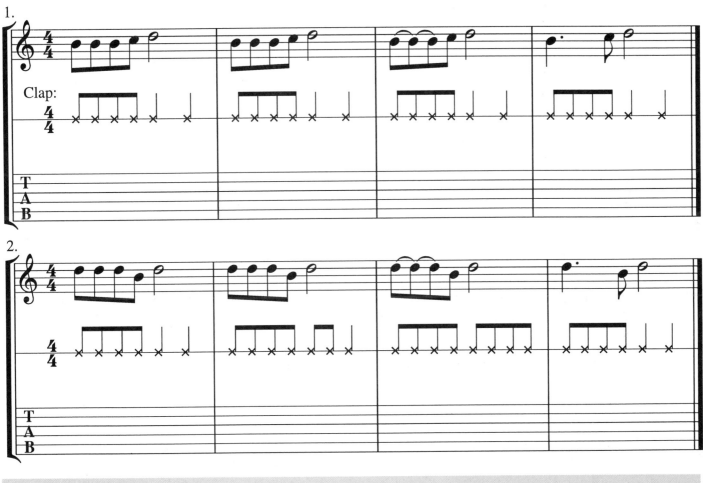

1.

2.

Teacher Tips, Student page 26:

- The brief introduction to scales and keys provided on student page 26 prepares students for viewing music in a structured, systematic manner. Notes will not be introduced randomly but within the framework of a scale. A broader understanding of scales will develop as major scales are compared with minor, pentatonic, and blues.

- In general, students should master the scale and chord progressions introduced at the beginning of a unit before playing the musical selections in the unit. When playing the scales together, play each tone twice in a scale. This allows the students to prepare their fingers, to correct themselves, and to catch up if they get lost. Scales should be played in this manner at the beginning of each class as a warm-up.

- Students may remain in I Position for all scales throughout the book other than A Major.

Activities, Student page 26:

- Review with students the definitions of **octave, interval, scale, major scale, half step, whole step, sharp, flat, key signature,** and **major key** provided on student page 26.

- As students' skills increase, the following variations on scale playing will make learning new scales interesting.

  1. Divide the class into two sections. Each section begins two notes (a third) later than the previous section. Divide the class further into three or four sections and repeat the activity.

  2. Divide the class into sections. Each section plays a different note value in the scale.

  3. Divide the class into sections. Each section plays a different rhythm on the same note.

  4. Have students experiment with getting louder and getting softer as they play.

  5. Conduct the class and have students observe your hand motions: slow down, speed up, stop in the middle, play softer, and play louder.

  6. Let a student take over the conducting.

6 – MAKING MUSIC: G MAJOR

For the remainder of this book, each unit will focus on a particular key and the corresponding scale in I Position. Chords based on the 1st, 4th, and 5th notes of the scale, called I, IV, and V7 chords respectively, will also be introduced. These are your most important chords in any key. Memorize them! Each unit also includes several tunes in the corresponding key. This unit focuses on the key of G Major.

An **OCTAVE** is the **INTERVAL** (pitch distance) between a note and the next higher or lower note with the same name.

A **SCALE** is a succession of notes ascending or descending from a given note to a note an octave higher or lower (the next note which has the same name). There are many types of scales, including major, minor, pentatonic, and blues.

A **MAJOR SCALE** is an eight-note scale which uses each note of the music alphabet. In a major scale, a **HALF STEP** (one fret on the guitar) appears between the third and fourth, and seventh and eighth notes of the scale. The interval between all other notes is a **WHOLE STEP** (two frets on the guitar).

In music, you sometimes see **SHARPS** (♯) and **FLATS** (♭). A sharp tells you to raise the corresponding pitch by one half step (one fret). A flat tells you to lower the corresponding pitch by one half step (one fret).

The sharps or flats located to the right of the clef are called a **KEY SIGNATURE**. The sharps or flats in a key signature affect all of the notes of the same letter name in the music. For example, a sharp written on the F line in the key signature means that all F's should be played as F♯'s.

Each key signature has a name which corresponds with a **MAJOR KEY**. Similarly, every major key has a corresponding major scale with the same name and same sharps or flats as the corresponding key signature.

G Major Scale

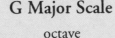

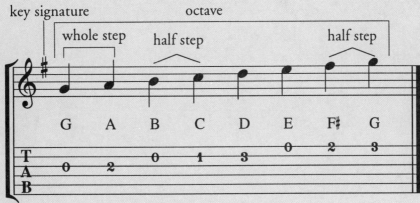

Teacher Tips, Student page 27:

- The G Major scale and chords are the most accessible on the guitar. Students may benefit from playing simplified versions of the C and G chords until they are ready to play the full chords. Students will willingly play full chords as they increase in skill.

- Not all of the musical selections in Unit 6 will be confined to the one-octave G Major scale that is bracketed. Notes beyond the one-octave G Major scale in I Position have therefore been provided on student page 27. However, when rehearsing the G Major scale with students, play the one-octave scale only, adding the other notes in I Position only when students are familiar with the one-octave scale. Playing the one-octave scale will help students to recognize the pattern of half and whole steps of a major scale and to feel the sense of resolution at the end of the scale.

- More musical selections are given in G Major than in any other key so that the students can gain confidence in their technique and playing.

- Remind students to move all of their fingers simultaneously when changing chords.

Warm-up, Student page 27:

- Review the meanings of major scale, sharp, and key signature with students.

Activities, Student page 27:

- Rehearse the G Major scale in class, playing each tone of the scale twice. This allows students the opportunity to listen and make corrections.

- Demonstrate the correct positions for playing the G, C, and D7 chords for students, and have students play the chords together.

- Review the definition of **chord progression**, **downstroke**, and **upstroke** provided on student page 27.

- Complete the *Practicing in G Major* exercise with the class. Eventually, students will be asked to learn scales, chords, and bass tones on their own, using chord progression patterns that they create. Completing this activity in class will help students learn how to practice new scales and keys.

- Incorporate rhythmic patterns introduced in the songs by playing them in the scales. For example, the dotted quarter and eighth note rhythm in *Michael, Row the Boat Ashore,* on student page 28, could be practiced by playing the first full measure of this song in a scale pattern:

 etc.

- Review the dotted quarter note value by asking one half of the class to play four quarter notes per scale tone while the other half plays the above pattern. Have students listen for the second quarter note (beat) before playing the eighth note.

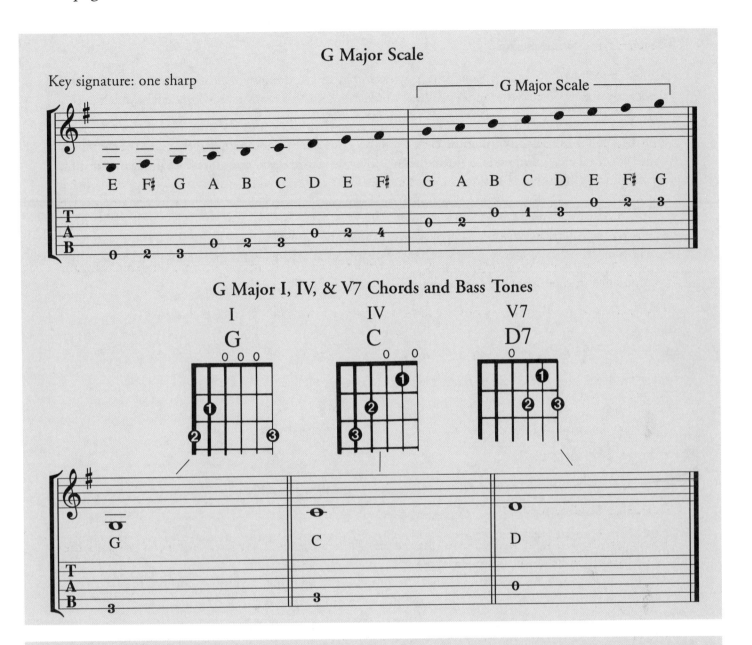

G Major Scale

Key signature: one sharp

G Major Scale

E F♯ G A B C D E F♯   G A B C D E F♯ G

G Major I, IV, & V7 Chords and Bass Tones

I	IV	V7
G	C	D7

A **CHORD PROGRESSION** is a sequence of two or more chords. Play chord progressions using a combination of **DOWNSTROKES** and **UPSTROKES**. Downstrokes (↓) are played by brushing the strings with the fingernails of the **i** or **m** fingers or the thumb (p) in a downward motion. Upstrokes (↑) are played by brushing the strings lightly with the thumbnail or with the **i** or **m** fingers in an upward motion. Remember to relax your right arm as you strum.

Practicing in G Major

1. Play each note of the G Major scale twice. Practice playing the scale from beginning to end in ascending and descending order, at first slowly and then more quickly. Then practice all of the notes in I Position in the key of G Major.

2. Practice G, C, and D7 chords individually at first, and then as part of a chord progression.

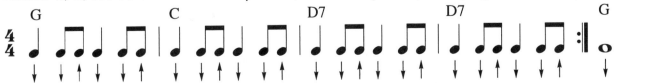

3. Practice the bass tones by playing one bass tone per measure to accompany the chord progression above.

Teacher Tips, Student page 28:

• Student tips for playing the melody, chord strumming, and bass lines are clearly marked and appear before most songs. Have students read these instructions carefully before playing each new song.

• For songs beginning with pick-up notes, students should always count one full measure in advance and then the measure containing the pick-up notes. Have chord and bass players enter on the first complete measure. Later, arrange introductions, having chord and bass players begin two or four measures in advance of the melody.

• Remind students to "play" the quarter rests by dampening the strings.

• The *Before You Play* checklist on student page 29 should be applied to each musical selection learned. It will train students to take a general survey of the material before beginning, and will help them to approach music intelligently and with a sense of structure.

Warm-up, Student page 28:

• Have students play the G Major scale, playing each tone twice.

Activities, Student page 28:

• Complete the *Before You Play* checklist on student page 29 with students for *Michael, Row the Boat Ashore*.

• Explain to students that the pick-up notes represent the last beats in a measure and are therefore unaccented.

• Ask these questions of students: What is the purpose of beginning a musical composition with a pick-up measure? Which beats are represented in the pick-up measure of *Michael, Row the Boat Ashore?* How many beats does the last measure of the song have? Why?

• Have students practice counting before beginning the pick-up measure. Count one full measure, and then the missing beats preceding the pick-up measure. In *Michael, Row the Boat Ashore*: 1 2 3 4 1 2....

Have one group clap the quarter note beats and count them aloud while the remainder of the class plays the melody.

• Once students have mastered the melody, practice the chords and bass tones with students. Then, divide the class in half, and have one group play the melody while the other group plays the chords or bass tones. Switch roles and repeat. Then, divide the class into three groups and assign each group a part. Rotate parts so that students have the opportunity to master each part.

Interdisciplinary Studies, Student page 28:

• Read the following cultural background on *Michael, Row the Boat Ashore* to students:

Michael, Row the Boat Ashore was originally a work song sung by African slaves in the southern United States in the mid-19th century. The steady rhythm of the song helped to maintain an even pace to the work. The song is performed in a call-and-response style: the first phrase of music is sung by a song leader, and the second phrase is a response from the rest of the singers.

Before playing any new song, complete a checklist like the one provided below *Kumbaya.*

PICK-UP NOTES are unaccented notes which come before the first complete measure of a piece. The pick-up notes and the notes in the last measure equal one complete measure.

Michael, Row the Boat Ashore and Kumbaya

Read the instructions below, and practice each as specified. Then, perform both songs with two other guitars, or with your entire class. Each player should be assigned a part: melody, chords, or bass.

| MELODY | Fill in the TAB for both songs. The first two notes of each song are pick-up notes. Count the first and second beats before beginning the song. |

| CHORDS | Use the following pattern for strumming the chord progressions accompanying each song, beginning on the first beat of the first complete measure: |

| BASS | Play the roots of the chords indicated in the music. In *Michael, Row the Boat Ashore*, play one tone on the first beat of each measure, except in the 7th complete measure, play two tones. In *Kumbaya*, play two tones per measure. |

Michael, Row the Boat Ashore

African-American Spiritual

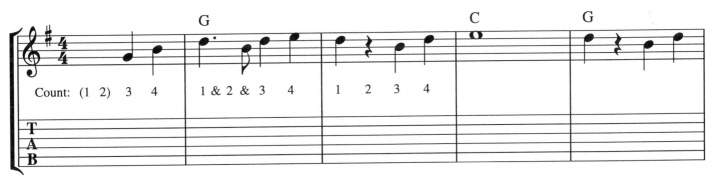

WG108T

Teacher Tip, Student page 29:

- Instruct students playing the bass tone accompaniment for *Kumbaya* to play a tone on the first beat of each measure and at each chord change, which often occurs on the third beat. Playing a bass tone while the melody has a tied note will assist melody players to count the full value of their tied notes.

Warm-up, Student page 29:

- Rehearse the G Major scale, playing each tone twice.

- Have students play *Michael, Row the Boat Ashore* (student page 28) three times, switching parts each time so everyone has a chance to play each part.

Activities, Student page 29:

- *Kumbaya* also begins with a pick-up measure of two quarter notes in $\frac{4}{4}$ time and has a dotted quarter rhythm in the first measure. Ask students to identify how long each of the tied notes are in the song.

- Complete the *Before You Play* checklist with students for *Kumbaya*. Have students play the melody in class together.

- To help students who are having difficulty playing the tied notes, have them clap the rhythm first.

- Ask students to think about how the long, tied notes are affecting the music. Have them play the song again, but shortening the tied notes to two beats each to see how the song is changed.

- Complement the included music with selections of your choice and/or of your students' choice that use the I–IV–V7 chord progression. A duplicable page of blank staff and TAB has been provided on page 158 for notating songs for students.

Interdisciplinary Studies, Student page 29:

- Read the following cultural background on *Kumbaya* to students:

Folk songs will often wander from culture to culture, changing in tempo or style along the way. One of the explanations for the origin of *Kumbaya* is that it is a folk song from Zimbabwe, a country in southeast Africa. *Kumbaya* would have been sung by a young Zimbabwean woman before her wedding, to mourn the ending of her youth. When the song was adopted in Europe and the United States, it became a more upbeat, uplifting tune.

Kumbaya

Zimbabwean Folk Song

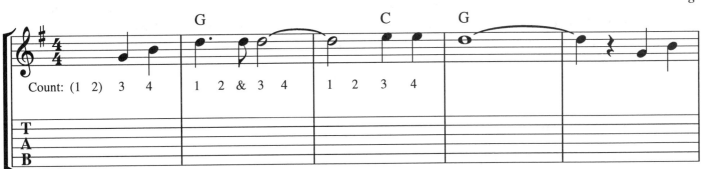

Count: (1 2) 3 4   1 2 & 3 4   1 2 3 4

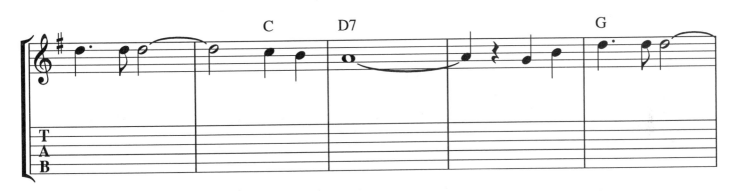

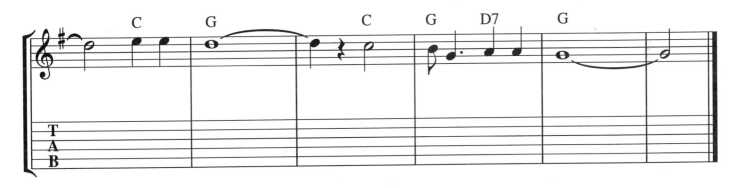

Before You Play

Identify:
- [ ] key signature
- [ ] time signature
- [ ] highest and lowest notes
- [ ] shortest and longest notes
- [ ] repeated rhythmic patterns
- [ ] phrases

Teacher Tip, Student pages 30–31:

- *Pavane* and *Galliard* will challenge the students' ability to play an unknown instrumental piece. The challenge will be to maintain a steady beat while playing the different note values. Not only the meter and basic rhythms are different, but the general character and expression of these sibling dances are different.

Warm-up, Student pages 30–31:

- Have students play the G Major scale, playing each tone twice.

- Ask students to choose one of the songs they have already learned, such as *Michael, Row the Boat Ashore* (student page 28) or *Kumbaya* (student page 29). Divide the class into three groups, and have each group play a part in the chosen song.

Activities, Student pages 30–31:

- Have students play the warm-up song again, but this time use hand gestures and actions to indicate where students should play softer and louder.

- Explain to students that the loudness or softness of music is called **dynamics**, and explain the meanings of *piano, forte, diminuendo,* and *crescendo*.

- Choose a song students are familiar with. Have one student direct the class when to play louder or softer, or when to play increasingly louder or softer. Have them use the new terms that they have learned to convey the information to the class. Repeat this activity with further songs.

- Read to students the information on *Pavane* and *Galliard* provided on student page 30.

- Have students explain the difference in feel between *Pavane*, in $\frac{4}{4}$ time, and *Galliard*, in $\frac{3}{4}$ time.

- Ask students to identify similarities and differences between *Pavane* and *Galliard* in terms of phrasing, repeated phrases, and note similarities.

- Practice the chord and bass line rhythm patterns with students.

- Rehearse *Pavane* and *Galliard* with students.

- *Pavane* and *Galliard* can be underscored with drums, tambourines, or other percussion instruments. The "tambora" technique on the guitar is played by tapping the bridge of the guitar. It creates a drum-like sound.

- Once students have become familiar with each piece, have them write in dynamic markings between the staff and TAB. Have students volunteer to tell the rest of the class when to play softer or louder, according to the dynamic markings they have written into their music.

• Duplicate and distribute the Evaluation Worksheet on page 159. Divide students into groups of five. Ask each student to perform the one-octave G Major scale, the G Major chord progression (student page 27), and one of the songs learned thus far in Unit 6. Have the other students in the group evaluate the performer based on the criteria provided on the worksheet.

Interdisciplinary Studies, Student pages 30–31:

• Read the following historical background for *Pavane* and *Galliard* to students:

Pavane and *Galliard* were composed during the Renaissance period in Europe (1400–1600). The Renaissance period was a time of increasing wealth in Europe. The nobility—kings, queens, and knights—would hold festivals where guests would feast and dance to music. Throughout the early Renaissance, music was often performed at these occasions on a lute, an early form of the guitar which is pear-shaped and has a rounded back.

In France, however, an instrument closer to the modern classic guitar was becoming more and more popular by the mid-1500s. This instrument, known as a five-course guitar, had ten strings, an elongated shape, and intricate decorations. As a result of the guitar's increasing popularity in France, dance music usually composed for the lute began to be composed for the guitar instead, such as Pierre Phalèse's *Pavane* and *Galliard*.

DYNAMICS indicate the degree of loudness. You can influence the character of a piece of music by playing loudly or softly during certain phrases in the music. Composers sometimes write **DYNAMIC MARKINGS**, such as the ones below, beneath a line of music so that you know where to play softly and where to play loudly.

p (piano) = soft   *dim. (diminuendo)* = become gradually softer

f (forte) = loud   *cresc. (crescendo)* = become gradually louder

Pavane and *Galliard*, published by Pierre Phalèse, were composed in the mid-1500s, when the guitar was very popular in Paris. They are **pair dances**—contrasting pieces associated with types of dance that draw from the same musical material. The *Pavane* is a slow, stately walking dance in $\frac{4}{4}$, while the lively *Galliard* is a lighter, hopping dance in $\frac{3}{4}$.

Pavane and Galliard

| MELODY | Fill in the TAB before playing. When playing each piece, be sure to give each half note, whole note, dotted half note, and dotted quarter note its full value so that you do not play too quickly. As you play, try to capture the spirit of each dance in your performance. After you become familiar with each piece, write in dynamic markings between the staff and TAB that help define the phrases. |

CHORDS

Pavane $\frac{4}{4}$ *Galliard* $\frac{3}{4}$
Strum: Strum:

BASS   Play the roots of the chords indicated in the music. Bass line rhythms:

Pavane: $\frac{4}{4}$ *Galliard:* $\frac{3}{4}$

Pavane

Pierre Phalèse (1510 – c.1573)

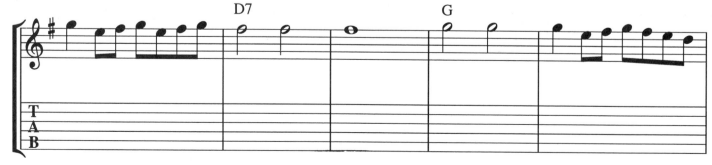

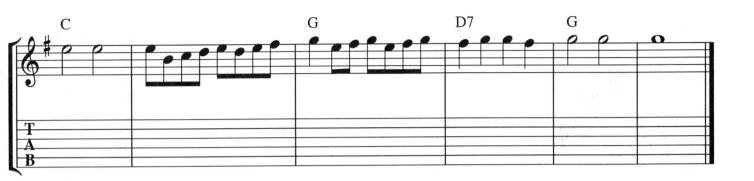

Galliard

Pierre Phalèse (1510 – c.1573)

Teacher Tips, Student page 32:

- $\frac{6}{8}$ can be counted in six beats per measure, but it is more commonly counted in two beats per measure. To help students become accustomed to $\frac{6}{8}$, the counting in *Irish Jig* has been written in six beats per measure. As students become familiar with this meter, have them begin feeling the meter in two beats per measure.

- Have students place their 3 and 1 fingers on the tones D and C (② string) in preparation for playing this quick tune.

Activities, Student page 32:

- Review with students the definition of $\frac{6}{8}$ time provided on student page 32.

- Divide the class into two groups. Have one group clap eighth notes while the other group claps dotted quarter notes. This activity will help students understand counting $\frac{6}{8}$ meter in two beats per measure.

- Have students use the *Before You Play* checklist from student page 29 for *Irish Jig*. Also ask students: How many open strings are played? How many notes are played using the left hand?

- Rehearse *Irish Jig* with students.

Interdisciplinary Studies, Student page 32:

- Read the following cultural background for *Irish Jig* to students:

Irish Jig is a traditional dance tune from Ireland. Ireland is an island off the coast of England. It is divided politically into the Republic of Ireland, an independent nation, and Northern Ireland, a territory of Great Britain. Dublin is the capital of the Republic of Ireland.

Ireland has a rich folk music heritage. Irish dance music is especially well known, and includes the fast, upbeat music of the jig, reel, and hornpipe. The people of Ireland sometimes gather to perform these traditional Irish dances and tell folk tales at celebrations known as *ceilidhe* (pronounced KAY-lee).

Irish ballads and folk songs are often sung to the accompaniment of the harp, fiddle, or flute. The Irish harp is smaller than harps used in modern concerts, and is triangular in shape. The harpist plucks the strings of the harp with the fingernails or fingertips.

Worksheet 5, Student page 32:

- The duplicable Worksheet 5 is provided on page 142. Worksheet 5 asks students to recognize $\frac{6}{8}$ time and to compose a short exercise in $\frac{6}{8}$ time. Students are then asked to listen to other students play their compositions, to notate the rhythms played, and to recognize the pattern of tones played.

$\frac{6}{8}$ is a time signature which indicates that there are six beats per measure and an eighth note gets one beat in a measure. Accents fall on the first and fourth of the six eighth notes in each measure.

6 beats per measure

an eighth note gets 1 beat

 Irish Jig

| MELODY | Fill in the TAB before you play. Remember to count the eighth notes before the pick-up. In the first, third, and fifth full measures, play the D on the open ④ string. |

| CHORDS | Strum: 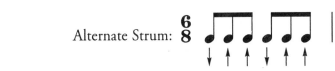 |

| BASS | Play the roots of the chords indicated in the music. Bass line rhythm: |

Irish Jig

Traditional Irish Dance

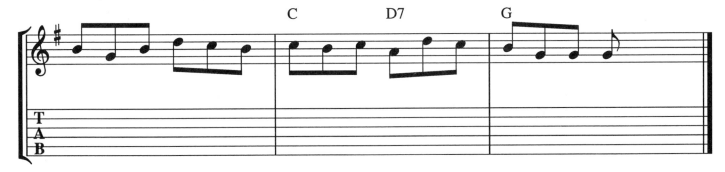

Teacher Tips, Student page 33:

- TAB lines have been omitted for the *Duet* and *Academic Festival March* to help students focus on the rhythms they are playing.

- In *Duet,* parts A and B both use only two different pitches. Part B is played only on open strings. Remind students to dampen the eighth rests with the fingers noted in parentheses. Explain to students that when repeating a phrase, it is better to use the same right hand fingering as used the first time. This guarantees a consistency of tone production. Often, as in this example, it will mean using the same finger twice (the last tone and the first tone are both played with the **m** finger).

- In *Academic Festival March,* parts A, B, and C all use the same tone material at the same time. The only difference lies in the eighth rests that are inserted in the B and C parts.

Warm-up, Student page 33:

- Have students play *A Moment of Silence* on student page 24 to reinforce playing music with rests.

Activities, Student page 33:

- Review with students the definition of **eighth rest** provided on student page 33.

- Complete the *Before You Play* checklist (student page 29) for *Duet* and *Academic Festival March* with students. Understanding the limited amount of musical elements that are presented in *Duet* and *Academic Festival March* will help students manage to play without TAB.

- To prepare students to play *Duet,* divide the class into two groups. Have one group clap part A of *Duet,* and have the other group clap part B. Switch roles and repeat the clapping activity. Then, have students play the duet together, one group playing part A and the other group playing part B. Students might also be helped when playing *Duet* by having some students clapping steady eighth notes.

- Rehearse *Academic Festival March* in the same manner as *Duet.*

- Divide students into groups of two, and have them complete the Unit 6 Review checklist to prepare them for the Unit 6 Quiz.

- *Academic Festival March* is an arrangement of a tune from *Academic Festival* Overture by Johannes Brahms. If you have a recording, share it with students. Have students raise their hands when the tune they recognize from *Academic Festival March* begins.

Interdisciplinary Studies, Student page 33:

- Read the following historical background for *Academic Festival March* to students:

Johannes Brahms (1833–1897) lived during the Romantic period (1820–1900) in Europe. Composers during the Romantic period used music to express their emotions and thoughts. Their music was non-traditional, making it difficult to play, with complex rhythms and long, flowing melodies.

Brahms was born in Hamburg, Germany to a musical family. His father taught him how to play the piano, and he was soon composing. When he was 46 years old, Brahms was offered an honorary doctorate degree from a university in Germany. The university expected him to write a musical composition in return for the degree. Brahms wrote his famous *Academic Festival* Overture for this occasion. Into this work he weaved songs that were popular with German college students. The melody found in *Academic Festival March* on student page 33 is based on "The Fox Song," which is heard about three-fourths of the way through Brahms' work, *Academic Festival* Overture.

Unit 6 Quiz, Student page 33:

- The duplicable Unit 6 Quiz is provided on pages 149–150. The Unit 6 Quiz tests students on the G Major scale and I, IV, and V7 chords, as well as octaves, sharps, flats, half steps, pick-ups, dynamics, $\frac{6}{8}$ time, and eighth rests.

γ = EIGHTH REST

An **EIGHTH REST** is as long as an eighth note.

Duet

Both *Duet* and *Academic Festival March* are written in staff notation only so that you can concentrate on playing the eighth rests. Write the counting in each part, then perform this duet with your class or with a partner. Count the eighth notes and rests carefully. Remember to dampen the vibrating string on each rest with your **i** or **m** finger as indicated.

Academic Festival March-Trio

Write the counting for each part, then practice each part. When each part has been mastered, perform parts A and B, then A, B, and C with two other guitarists or with your entire class. Listen carefully to the rhythms of the other parts as you play.

Academic Festival March

Johannes Brahms (1833–1897)
arr. Bruce Pearson

Unit 6 Review

Identify:
- [ ] octave
- [ ] interval
- [ ] scale
- [ ] major scale
- [ ] half step
- [ ] whole step
- [ ] sharp
- [ ] flat
- [ ] key signature
- [ ] major key
- [ ] G Major scale
- [ ] G Major I, IV, V7 chords
- [ ] chord progression
- [ ] downstroke/upstroke
- [ ] pick-up note
- [ ] dynamics
- [ ] *piano*
- [ ] *forte*
- [ ] *diminuendo*
- [ ] *crescendo*
- [ ] $\frac{6}{8}$ time
- [ ] eighth rest

Perform:
- [ ] *Michael, Row the Boat Ashore*
- [ ] *Kumbaya*
- [ ] *Pavane* and *Galliard*
- [ ] *Irish Jig*
- [ ] *Academic Festival March*

Teacher Tips, Student page 34:

- The one-octave C Major scale in I Position traverses the four middle strings of the guitar. It should be played with the alternating rest stroke with the right hand fingers. The right forearm must move from the elbow as the strings are traversed, in order to ensure a consistent tone quality.

- Learning to play scales is essential to developing students' technical and musical ability. Playing scales exercises the fingers, creating strength, dexterity, speed, and precision. Playing scales also helps students to hear a composition's **tonality** (tones that belong together) and to become familiar with systems of tones on the fingerboard.

- Explain to students that scales can be played a variety of different ways on the guitar fingerboard. This one-octave C Major scale pattern in I Position is just one of many possible ways of playing C Major.

Warm-up, Student page 34:

- Have students play *Hush, Little Baby* (student page 19) and *Down in the Valley* (student page 20) to remind them of the key of C Major.

Activities, Student page 34:

- Ask students to identify the C Major key signature.

- The C and G7 chords should not be difficult for students to master. Have students compare these extended forms of the C and G7 chords with the simple forms on student page 21. Note how the tones in the simple forms are contained within the extended forms. Explain to students that these chords produce the same sound, but they include doubling. **Doubling** means that tones appear more than once in a single chord.

- Explain and demonstrate for students how to play the F chord. The ① and ② strings will be held down simultaneously with the 1 finger of the left hand. This finger must lie flat over the two strings. This technique is known as a **partial barre** and serves as a preparation for the more complicated barre chords that students will learn as more advanced guitar players.

- Complete the *Practicing in C Major* activity with students.

7—MAKING MUSIC: C MAJOR

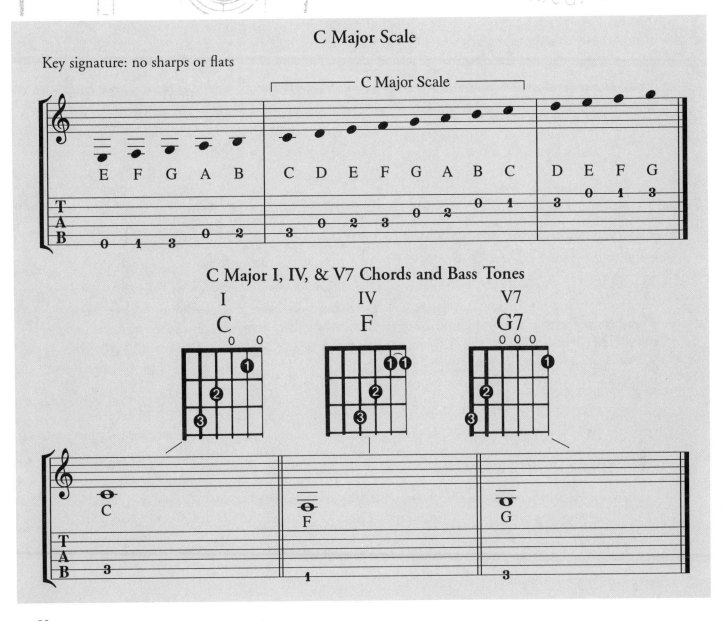

C Major Scale

Key signature: no sharps or flats

C Major Scale

E F G A B   C D E F G A B C   D E F G

C Major I, IV, & V7 Chords and Bass Tones

I	IV	V7
C	F	G7

C   F   G

Practicing in C Major

1. Play each note of the C Major scale twice. Practice playing the scale from beginning to end in ascending and descending order, at first slowly and then more quickly. Then practice all of the notes in I Position in the key of C Major.

2. Practice C, F, and G7 chords individually at first, and then as part of a chord progression.

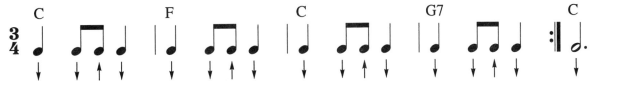

C   F   C   G7   C

3. Practice the bass tones by playing one bass tone per measure to accompany the chord progression above.

Teacher Tips, Student page 35:

- *Lullaby for Two Little Stars* is in $\frac{3}{4}$ time and introduces the quarter/dotted quarter/eighth note rhythm.

- Explain to students that both the G Major chord and the G7 chord appear in the piece. Remind students that they learned the G Major chord on student page 27. An explanation of this occurrence is not included in the student edition in order to maintain the consistent I–IV–V7 pattern that students learn in each major key. For more advanced students, this may be a good opportunity to introduce the concept of the 7th chord as a chord that leads back to the I chord.

- The lyrics to *Lullaby for Two Little Stars* in the original German, as well as in English translation, are provided below to reinforce the word-rhythm association. The German lyrics can be used as an opportunity to work with a German class in learning this song.

Activities, Student page 35:

- Have students practice counting and clapping the quarter/dotted quarter/eighth note rhythm in *Lullaby for Two Little Stars*. Then, have students rehearse the melody together. When they have mastered the melody, divide the students into three groups to play the melody, chords, and bass lines. Switch roles and repeat.

- After students have mastered *Lullaby for Two Little Stars*, duplicate and distribute the Evaluation Worksheet on page 159. Divide students into groups of five. Ask each student to perform the one-octave C Major scale, the C Major chord progression (student page 34), and *Lullaby for Two Little Stars*. Have the other students in the group evaluate the performer based on the criteria provided on the worksheet. This activity could be alternatively completed later in Unit 7.

Interdisciplinary Studies, Student page 35:

- The original German text to *Lullaby for Two Little Stars* by Grant Gustafson:

Jantje und Leffe, zwei Sternelein,
Fliegt durch den Himmel, teilt Träumelein;
Jantje und Leffe, funkelt mir zu,
Über den Wolken, schlafet in Ruh'.
Jantje und Leffe, zwei Brüderlein,
Schlaft mit den Engeln, nimmer allein.

Translation:

Jantje and Leffe, two little stars,
Fly through the heavens, share little dreams;
Jantje and Leffe, twinkle to me,
Above the clouds, sleep in peace.
Jantje and Leffe, two little brothers,
Sleep with the angels, never alone.

Lullaby for Two Little Stars

MELODY	Wait for the third beat before playing the last eighth note in the measures that include:

For more precise playing, count eighth notes:

1   2   3 &   1 & 2 & 3 &

CHORDS	Play the G chord from the G Major section instead of G7 when indicated.

Strum:

BASS	Bass line rhythm:

Lullaby for Two Little Stars
(for Jan and Leif)

Grant Gustafson

C   G   F   G

F   C   F   C   F

C   G   G7   C   G

F   G   C   G   F   G7   C

Teacher Tips, Student page 36:

• *Simple Gifts* is in the key of C Major. It is played in this version on the top three strings (①, ②, ③).

• The I–V7 cadence (C–G7) should be familiar to students. Have students practice the full chords and analyze the movement between them. Watch that students lift all fingers off the fingerboard simultaneously when changing chords, and place them down on the new chord at the same time.

Warm-up, Student page 36:

• Reinforce rests by having students play *Academic Festival March* (student page 33). This piece will prepare students to play the eighth rests that appear in *Simple Gifts*.

Activities, Student page 36:

• Have students identify which other songs they have learned which use these notes (*Hush, Little Baby* and *Down in the Valley*). Have students verify that all these tunes are in C Major.

• Have students fill in the TAB, and then rehearse the melody together as a class. When students have mastered the tune, divide the class into three groups to play the three parts. Switch roles and repeat.

• For students who are having difficulty with the rhythm in *Simple Gifts*, have them count out loud as they play.

• *Simple Gifts* can also be played within the range of the one-octave C Major scale on student page 34 by **transposing** the melody down one octave, and using the low G tone on the ⑥ string for the pick-up notes. More advanced students can be encouraged to transpose *Simple Gifts* down an octave, and accompany the rest of the class as they play the song as written.

• Explain to students that variations on the melody of *Simple Gifts* were incorporated into the end of a ballet entitled *Appalachian Spring*, written by American composer Aaron Copland (1900–1990) in 1944. *Appalachian Spring* helped to make *Simple Gifts* a widely recognized and loved song. If you have a recording of *Appalachian Spring*, share it with students. Ask students to raise their hands when they hear the melody of *Simple Gifts* begin.

Interdisciplinary Studies, Student page 36:

• Read the following historical background for *Simple Gifts* to students:

Simple Gifts was originally a traditional song of a religious group in the United States known as the "Shakers." During the 19th century, the Shakers lived in tight-knit communities scattered around the eastern United States. They believed in the importance of hard work and a simple lifestyle. They manufactured their own plain, functional furniture for their homes, a style now known as Shaker which is popular today. The Shakers also enjoyed singing and dancing, and *Simple Gifts* was one of the many dance-tunes they composed. Although there are few members left in the society, the Shakers will be long remembered for their rich musical tradition and austere manner of living.

Simple Gifts

MELODY

Count eighth notes before the pick-up notes. Play the eighth rests as you did on page 33.

Like *Hush, Little Baby* and *Down in the Valley* (page 21), *Simple Gifts* can be accompanied by using only the C and G7 chords. Use either the simple versions of the chords shown on page 21, or the versions shown on page 34.

CHORDS

Strum: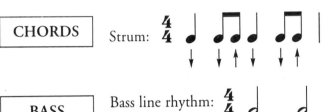

BASS

Bass line rhythm:

Simple Gifts

Shaker Tune

Teacher Tips, Student page 37:

• Like *Simple Gifts*, *Minuet* is played on the upper three strings of the guitar. Since there is no accompaniment, students can focus on playing the melody in unison.

• Although musical forms will not be formally introduced in this book, students' musical understanding can be enhanced by providing them with a general explanation of the form of a piece. Ask students to identify the phrases in *Minuet*, and to determine which phrases occur more than once. Explain to students that this piece takes a musical form or pattern of A – B – A – B1.

Activities, Student page 37:

• Review with students the definition of **natural** provided on student page 37. Explain the purpose of a sharp, flat, or natural in a measure, and be sure that students understand how to play the C♯ and C♮ in the 8th measure of *Minuet*.

• Have students fill in the TAB for *Minuet*. Rehearse the piece with students, emphasizing the importance of playing accurate rhythms and pitches so that there is one unified sound.

• Complete the Unit 7 Review checklist with students. Have students perform as a group the C Major scale, the C Major I, IV, and V7 chords and bass tones, *Simple Gifts*, *Lullaby for Two Little Stars*, and *Minuet*. The Evaluation Worksheet on page 159 could also be duplicated and distributed to test students' ability on the scale, chords, and a musical selection from the unit.

Interdisciplinary Studies, Student page 37:

• Read the following historical background for *Minuet* to students:

Minuet is an unaccompanied solo composition by Spanish guitarist-composer Fernando Sor (1778–1839). It is the first of his *Easy Etudes*, op. 60. Fernando Sor lived during the Classical period in Europe (1750–1820). Music of the Classical period emphasized simplicity, balance, and clarity. Unlike the emotionally expressive music of the later Romantic period, Classical music was often written in prescribed forms or structures. Famous Classical composers include Ludwig van Beethoven (1770–1827) and Wolfgang Amadeus Mozart (1756–1791).

During his lifetime, Fernando Sor was known as the "Beethoven of the Guitar," but he also composed music for other instruments and for voice. Along with the Italian composer Mauro Giuliani, Sor was the leading performer and composer of the "classical" guitar. He traveled widely, performing his music, and was admired in France, England, and Russia. He wrote over 65 works for the guitar, and his guitar method was to influence future generations of guitar players in the years to come.

Unit 7 Quiz, Student page 37:

• The duplicable Unit 7 Quiz is provided on page 151. The Unit 7 Quiz tests students on the C Major scale and I, IV, and V7 chords, as well as half steps, whole steps, sharps, flats, and naturals.

When a sharp (♯) or flat (♭) appears before a note in a composition, the note should be raised (♯) or lowered (♭) a half step (one fret). The sharp or flat is valid for the duration of the measure unless a **NATURAL** (♮) appears, which cancels a sharp or flat. A natural can also be used to cancel a sharp or flat in the key signature for the duration of the measure in which it appears.

Minuet

MELODY	Play *Minuet* without accompaniment. A new note, C♯ on the ② string, appears in the 8th measure. The TAB for this note has already been completed.

Minuet

Fernando Sor (1778–1839)

Unit 7 Review

Identify:
☐ C Major Scale
☐ C Major I, IV, V7 chords
☐ natural

Perform:
☐ *Simple Gifts*
☐ *Lullaby for Two Little Stars*
☐ *Minuet*

Teacher Tip, Student page 38:

- Remind students that while in I Position the left hand fingers correspond to the numbers of the frets expressed on the TAB, but in other positions they do not.

Activities, Student page 38:

- Have students identify which notes are affected by the two sharps in the key signature of D Major.

- Demonstrate the D, G, and A7 chords for students and have them strum the chords along with you.

- Complete the *Practicing in D Major* exercise with students in class.

- Have students learn to play the one-octave D Major scale in both I and II Positions, using open strings. In I Position, the E on the ④ string will be played with the 2 finger of the left hand and the F♯ with the 4 finger. In II Position, the E will be played with the 1 finger and the F♯ with the 3 finger.

- To prepare students for the chord strum pattern in *El Noy de la Mare* (student page 39), have students use this alternate meter and rhythm when practicing the D, G, and A7 chord progression on student page 38:

- To prepare students for the rhythm in *El Noy de la Mare*, introduce students to these clapping exercises. In Spain and Latin America, music is often accompanied with different kinds of clapping.

  seca = loud clap   Cup both hands and clap loudly.

  sorda = soft clap   Clap the fingertips of one hand into the lower palm of the other.

Have students clap steady eighth notes in ¾ time using loud claps. Then, have students clap steady eighth notes in ¾ time using soft claps. Then combine loud and soft claps, having students create loud claps on beat 1 and the & of beat 2, so the pattern of claps would be: "loud – soft – soft – loud – soft – soft." This rhythm prepares students for playing *El Noy de la Mare*, since the loud beats fall on the dotted quarter and on the eighth note in the majority of the measures. To challenge students, assign different claps to two or three different groups, requiring students to listen to one another and to experience musical interdependence.

8—*MAKING MUSIC: D MAJOR*

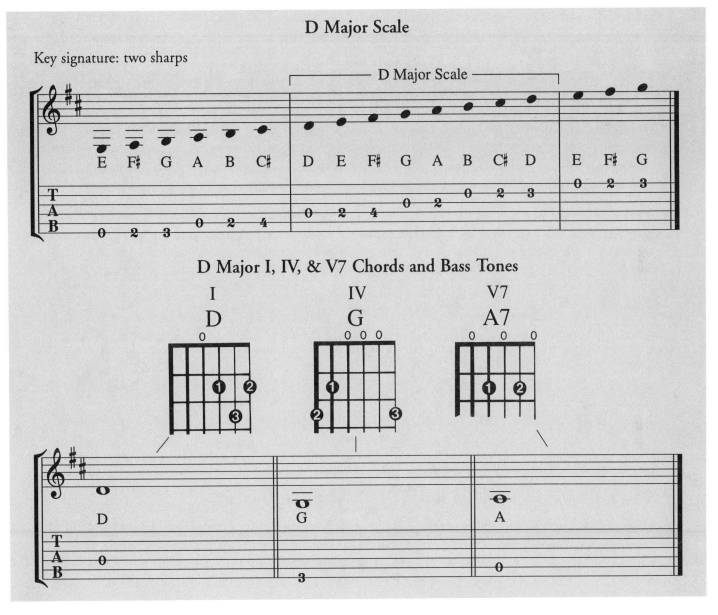

D Major Scale

Key signature: two sharps

D Major I, IV, & V7 Chords and Bass Tones

 Practicing in D Major

1. Play each note of the D Major scale twice. Practice playing the scale from beginning to end in ascending and descending order, at first slowly and then more quickly. Then practice all of the notes in I Position in the key of D Major.

2. Practice D, G, and A7 chords individually at first, and then as part of a chord progression.

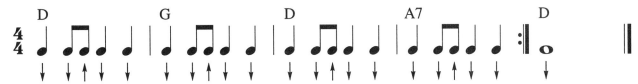

3. Practice the bass tones by playing one bass tone per measure to accompany the chord progression above.

Warm-up, Student page 39:

- To reinforce students' ability to play the D Major scale, have students play each note three times, accenting the first note of each group. Have them crescendo while ascending, decrescendo while descending. Students may also wish to play the scale in a round, or to do other scale activities listed on page 52.

Activities, Student page 39:

- To prepare students to play *El Noy de la Mare*, have students play the three-note rhythmic motif of *El Noy de la Mare* on each tone of the D Major scale.

- Have students analyze *El Noy de la Mare* before filling in the TAB or trying to play it on the guitar. Ask students to identify the key, the highest and lowest notes, and how many measures make up a phrase. Ask students to identify the smallest rhythmic unit that repeats itself in the piece. Explain to students that this rhythm is a **motif**.

- Have students practice playing the chord accompaniments provided in conjunction with *El Noy de la Mare* together. The alternate strum pattern requires that students slap the strings lightly against the fingerboard on the eighth note of the rhythm pattern. The percussive effect enhances the Spanish sound of the song. Have half of the students playing the chord accompaniment play the alternate strum.

- Rehearse the melody of *El Noy de la Mare* with students in class. Once they have mastered the melody, have students play *El Noy de la Mare* in II Position, using open strings. It is not only easier, but it will prepare the students to play the upcoming A Major scale (student page 43).

- Divide the class into three groups, and assign a part to each group. Switch roles and repeat.

Interdisciplinary Studies, Student page 39:

- Read the following cultural background of *El Noy de la Mare* to students:

El Noy de la Mare comes from a region in Spain called Catalonia. Catalonia, the birthplace of Fernando Sor, lies in the northeastern corner of Spain. Barcelona, on the Mediterranean coast, is the capital of Catalonia. Since Catalonia was traded many times between France and Spain, the Catalan language and culture is a unique combination of both French and Spanish influences.

Flamenco is one of the most famous dance and music forms in Spain. Flamenco music originated in Andalucia, a region in southern Spain, and includes singing, guitar music with the Flamenco guitar (see student page 2), and dancing. Women dancers wear brightly colored dresses and play *castanets* as they dance, while the men stomp their feet and shout.

El Noy de la Mare

MELODY The rhythm is structured in repeated four-measure phrases: the  rhythm progresses for three measures, then is slowed down in the fourth with longer notes. Wait for the second beat before playing the eighth note after a dotted quarter note. Count eighth notes throughout for more precise playing.

CHORDS Strum:  Alternate Strum: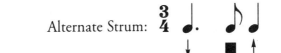

* Slap the strings against the fingerboard with the fingers before playing an upstroke.

BASS Bass line rhythm:

El Noy de la Mare

Catalan Carol

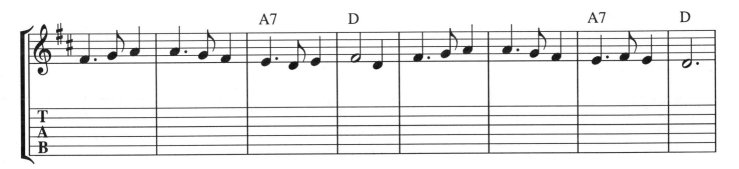

Teacher Tips, Student page 40:

- Effective group music-making requires rhythmic precision. By now, students should be aware of the importance of maintaining a steady beat while playing a piece of music. As more complex rhythms are introduced, such as the dotted eighth and sixteenth note rhythms on student pages 40 and 41, students should be reminded to count carefully and to think mathematically while maintaining a sense of the beat.

- Point out to students that the *Sixteenth Note Scale Exercise* progresses through an ascending and descending D Major scale. When students have mastered the D Major scale, they will play more comfortably and will be able to concentrate on the rhythms to be played.

- In *Listen to the Mockingbird,* the rhythms in parts A and B are played at different times and complement one another. This will pose a challenge to students and will require precise counting and listening.

Activities, Student page 40:

- Review with students the definition of **sixteenth notes** provided on student page 40.

- Divide the class into two groups and have one group play the melody of *Sixteenth Note Scale Exercise* while the other group claps the rhythm indicated. Percussions (tapping with fingertips on the side of the guitar) can also be substituted for the clapping line.

- Have students complete the *Before You Play* checklist on student page 29 for *Listen to the Mockingbird.*

- To prepare students to play *Listen to the Mockingbird,* have them write in the counting in each part, and then practice each part on an open single string.

- Have students master both part A and part B of *Listen to the Mockingbird* before dividing into groups to play the duet.

Interdisciplinary Studies, Student page 40:

- Read the following historical background for *Listen to the Mockingbird* to students:

Listen to the Mockingbird was written in 1855 by an American music publisher and composer named Septimus Winner (1827–1902). Winner was a largely self-taught musician, and by the age of 20 he had mastered the guitar, banjo, and violin.

One day Winner heard a young boy whistling the song of a mockingbird, and he was inspired to write a song based on the tune. This song was called *Listen to the Mockingbird,* and it became so popular that millions of copies of the song were sold in the United States and Europe within 50 years. Winner published the song under one of his pseudonyms, or pen names, Alice Hawthorne.

Sixteenth Note Scale Exercise

In the exercise below, write the counting. The counting for the first measure has been completed for you. As you play, count sixteenth notes aloud, carefully observing the right hand fingering indications.

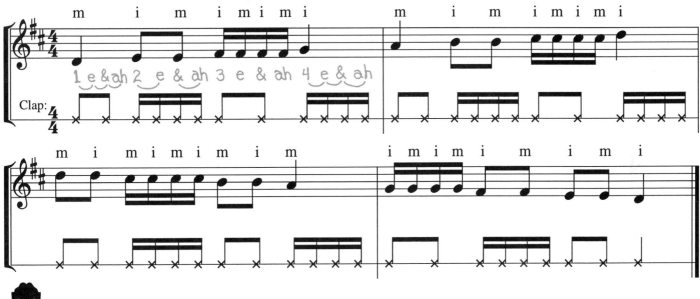

Listen to the Mockingbird – Duet

Write the counting in each part, then perform this duet with your class or with a partner. Count the sixteenth notes carefully.

Listen to the Mockingbird

Alice Hawthorne (1827–1902)

Teacher Tip, Student page 41:

• Help students to understand the dotted eighth and sixteenth note rhythm combination in terms of the relative distribution of the two notes over the space of one beat by explaining that the first note is long and the second note is much shorter. Students may benefit from feeling the short, sixteenth note as coming directly before the following beat.

Activities, Student page 41:

• Review with students the definitions of **sixteenth note, dotted eighth note,** and **dotted eighth/sixteenth note combination** provided on student page 41.

• Divide students into two groups, and have one group clap the top line of the example in the box at the top of the page, and the other group clap the bottom line. Say the counting out loud to help students feel this rhythm.

• Remind students to subdivide the dotted eighth note into its smallest common denominator, sixteenth notes, when playing *Single String Dance.*

• Divide the class into two groups, and have one group play the top line of *Single String Dance* and the other group clap the rhythm of the second line. Once students are accustomed to the rhythm, add the chords and bass lines (the second and third lines).

• Play for students examples of recorded music to reinforce the dotted eighth/sixteenth note combination.

• Duplicate and distribute the Evaluation Worksheet on page 159 of the Teacher's Edition. Divide students into groups of five. Ask each student to perform the one-octave D Major scale, the D Major chord progression (student page 38), and one of the songs learned thus far in Unit 8. Have the other students in the group evaluate the performer based on the criteria provided on the worksheet. This activity could be alternatively completed after students have mastered the last musical selection in the unit, *Alouette* (student page 42).

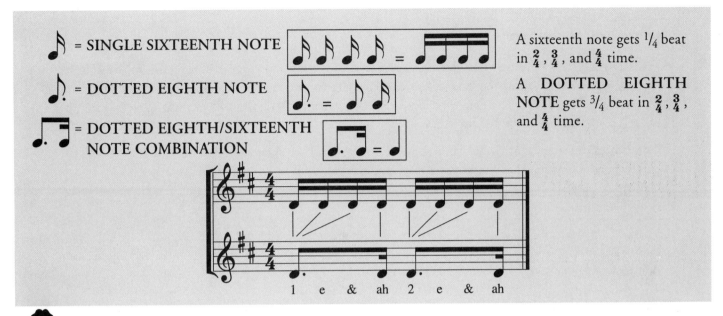

 Single String Dance

MELODY — Write the counting in the exercise below. The first two measures have been completed for you. As you play, listen to the chord accompaniment, and carefully observe the right hand fingering indications.

CHORDS — The chord progression and strum rhythm are provided on the second line below the melody.

Use the following strum pattern:

Play this quick strum pattern by supporting your thumb (**p**) on the ⑥ string and playing the up and downstrokes with your **m** finger.

BASS — The bass line is provided on the third line below the melody and chords.

WG108T

Teacher Tips, Student page 42:

- The dotted eighth/sixteenth note combination in *Alouette* lends a gracefulness to the melody. In a song of this nature, students should feel the lilting movement of the melody when playing the rhythm. The first note (dotted eighth note) in the beat is long, while the second note (sixteenth note) is short and comes directly before the next beat.

- The dotted quarter/eighth note combination also appears in *Alouette*. Remind students to count eighth notes silently if they are rushing this rhythmic pattern.

- The lyrics to *Alouette* in the original French have been included in order to reinforce the word-rhythm association. Some students may already be familiar with the song and the words. For those who are not, learning the words to a song in an unfamiliar language will help develop their appreciation for other cultures. The words can also be used as an opportunity to work with a French class in learning this song.

Activities, Student page 42:

- Have students fill in the TAB for *Alouette*. Rehearse the two strumming and bass line rhythm patterns with the class, having students count out loud as they play.

- Divide the class into two groups. Have one group play the melody for *Alouette* while the other group claps steady sixteenth notes. Switch roles, and this time have the clapping group say the counting syllables out loud to aid students playing the melody.

- Once students are familiar with the song, have them indicate dynamic markings for the song. Ask for volunteers to perform the song for the class, observing the dynamics they have indicated.

- Explain to students that "alouette" is the French word for "lark," a kind of bird. The words to the song speak of plucking the feathers off of the bird, perhaps to prepare it for a feast.

- Complete the Unit 8 Review checklist with the class.

Interdisciplinary Studies, Student page 42:

- Read the following cultural background for *Alouette* to students:

Alouette is a French-Canadian folk song. Canada is a large country which lies to the north of the United States. Ottawa is the capital of Canada.

French-speaking Canadians make up about a third of the population of Canada. Many French-Canadian folk songs were first sung by *voyageurs*—men who rowed large canoes around the vast water routes of Canada carrying goods for trade during the late 18th and early 19th century. Their journeys were long and difficult, so the men would sing upbeat tunes to accompany the paddling of the canoe. It is believed that the voyageurs could sing from memory as many as 40 or 50 songs with 50 to 60 verses apiece.

Unit 8 Quiz, Student page 42:

- The duplicable Unit 8 Quiz is provided on page 152. The Unit 8 Quiz tests students on the one-octave D Major scale and I, IV, and V7 chords, as well as sixteenth notes.

Alouette

| MELODY | In a lively tempo (speed), it is not always possible to carefully count sixteenth notes while playing dotted eighth/sixteenth note rhythms. In the following song, play the dotted eighth note long, and then play the sixteenth note right before the following beat. |

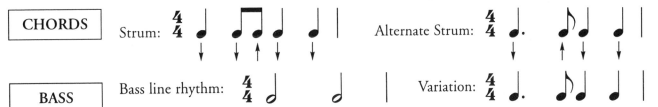

Alouette

Lively

French-Canadian Folk Song

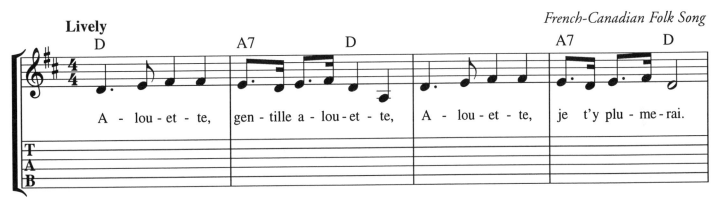

A - lou - et - te, gen - tille a - lou - et - te, A - lou - et - te, je t'y plu - me - rai.

Je t'y plu - me - rai la tête, Je t'y plu - me - rai la tête, Ah! la tête, Ah! la tête, A - lou - ette, A - lou - ette,

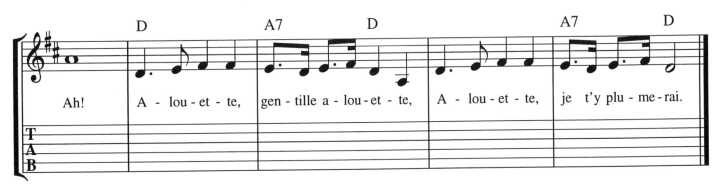

Ah! A - lou - et - te, gen - tille a - lou - et - te, A - lou - et - te, je t'y plu - me - rai.

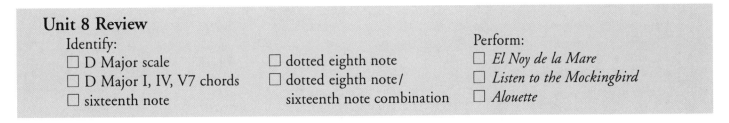

Unit 8 Review

Identify:

- ☐ D Major scale
- ☐ D Major I, IV, V7 chords
- ☐ sixteenth note
- ☐ dotted eighth note
- ☐ dotted eighth note/ sixteenth note combination

Perform:

- ☐ *El Noy de la Mare*
- ☐ *Listen to the Mockingbird*
- ☐ *Alouette*

Teacher Tips, Student page 43:

- The A Major scale can be played in II Position with open strings. It can also be played *without* using any open strings at all. The one-octave A Major scale in II Position is provided on student page 43 with and without open strings. For the scale without open strings, open string notes B and E are now played with the left hand. B is now located on the ③ string, 4th fret, and E on the ② string, 5th fret.

- The A Major scale in II Position without open strings is a movable (**transposable**) scale. In other words, the finger pattern that students learn while playing this scale can be shifted into any position on the guitar, changing the key. For example, the C Major scale can be played starting on the 5th fret, and the D Major scale starting on the 7th fret. More advanced students may be encouraged to try playing these scales using the transposable finger pattern.

- Explain to students that guitarists need to know how to transpose because it affects the sound of the piece being played, it makes it possible to play with other instrumentalists who are limited in their key possibilities, and it makes it possible to accompany singers in the key most comfortable for them.

- More advanced students should learn the three basic methods for **transposing** melodies from one key to another on the guitar:

  1. Learn each scale pattern individually and be able to play these with ease.

  2. Learn "transposable" scale patterns (those without open strings) and slide these into new positions.

  3. Use a **capo** to change the pitch of the entire guitar. A capo is a wood or metal bar that is placed on the guitar neck behind a fret in order to shorten the strings and thus change the pitch of the strings.

Activities, Student page 43:

- Have students practice shifting by playing the A Major scale in I Position. Explain to students that in order to reach the A on the ① string, students will have to shift from I Position to II Position. Students may find it easier to shift while playing the E on the open ① string. Thus, students would play open E, F♯ with the 1 finger, G♯ with the 3 finger, and A with the 4 finger.

- Demonstrate the A, D, and E7 chords for students, and have students strum the chords along with you.

- Have students choose a chord strum pattern and a chord progression from a previous key, such as *Practicing in D Major* (student page 38), to practice the A Major chords and bass tones.

- More advanced students should be encouraged to transpose *El Noy de la Mare* (student page 39) one octave higher, using the scale fingering pattern of A Major in II Position without open strings. The first tone of the piece is the F♯ on the ② string with the 1 finger in VII Position.

9 – MAKING MUSIC: A MAJOR

A Major Scale
in II Position with Open Strings

Key signature: three sharps

A Major Scale
in II Position without Open Strings

A Major I, IV, & V7 Chords and Bass Tones

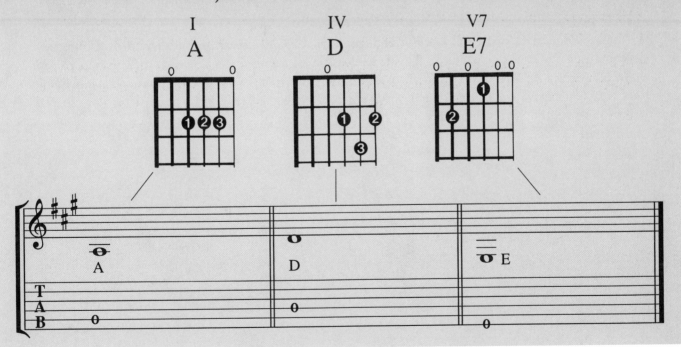

Teacher Tips, Student pages 44–45:

• *Ramblin'* is an example of a piece in $\frac{5}{4}$, which is a combination of $\frac{3}{4}$ and $\frac{2}{4}$ time.

• *Ramblin'* not only introduces $\frac{5}{4}$ time, but also demonstrates the concept of consonance and dissonance in music once *Ramblin' Accompaniment* is added.

Activities, Student pages 44–45:

• Review with students the definition of $\frac{5}{4}$ time provided on student page 44. Ask students: If $\frac{2}{4}$ and $\frac{4}{4}$ times are like walking or marching, and $\frac{3}{4}$ time is like skipping or waltzing, what kind of movement does $\frac{5}{4}$ time represent? Have students find a body movement that gives expression to $\frac{5}{4}$ time, with emphasis only on the first and fourth beats, such as swaying to the right for three beats, to the left for two. The movement should be kept smooth.

• Have students clap quarter notes in $\frac{5}{4}$ time. Place accents on the first and fourth beats, so that the measure is divided into two groups: the first with three quarter notes, the second with two quarter notes.

• Have students play the A Major scale in $\frac{5}{4}$ time. Have students play three quarter notes on the first note of the scale, two quarter notes on the second note, etc.

• Rehearse *Ramblin'* with the melody, chords, and bass lines indicated on student page 44.

• Once students have mastered the arrangement provided on student page 44, divide the class in half and have one group play *Ramblin'* while the other group plays *Ramblin' Accompaniment*. Ask students to identify moments in the song when the two parts seem to clash, and explain the difference between **consonance** and **dissonance**.

• Have students play scales in different intervals. Divide the class into any number of groups, and have students play the same scale, starting at different points to create different intervals. Discuss which intervals are consonant and which are dissonant.

• To reinforce students' aural understanding of consonance, have students play an arrangement of *Michael, Row the Boat Ashore* (student page 28) by creating a countermelody at intervals of thirds or sixths from the melody line. More advanced students could be involved in creating the arrangement themselves.

• After students have mastered *Ramblin'* and *Ramblin' Accompaniment*, duplicate and distribute the Evaluation Worksheet on page 159. Divide students into groups of five. Ask each student to perform the one-octave A Major scale, an A Major chord progression of the student's choice, and the melody of *Ramblin'*. Have the other students in the group evaluate the performer based on the criteria provided on the worksheet. This activity could be alternatively completed after students have mastered *Cantabile* (student pages 46–47).

$\frac{5}{4}$ is a time signature which indicates that there are five beats per measure and a quarter note gets one beat in a measure.

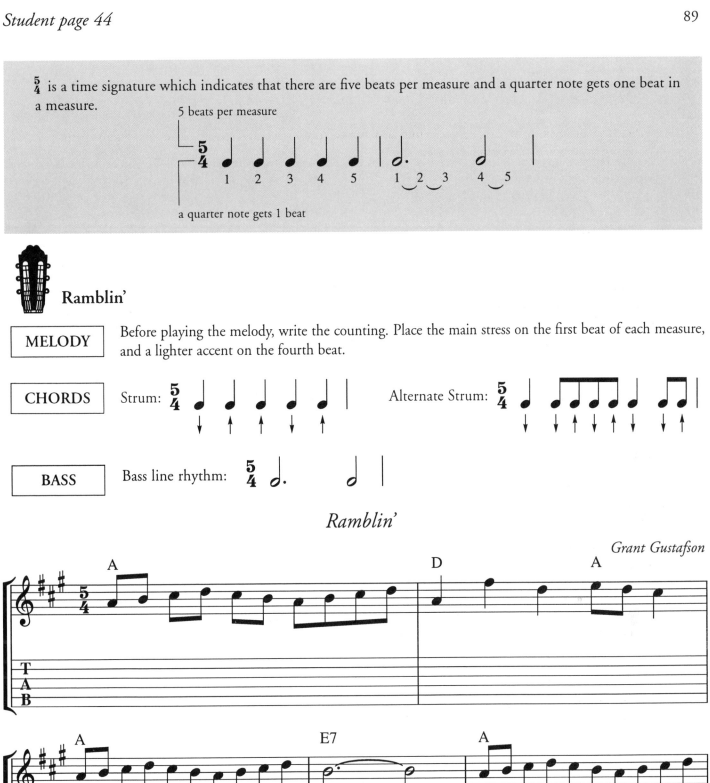

Ramblin'

| MELODY | Before playing the melody, write the counting. Place the main stress on the first beat of each measure, and a lighter accent on the fourth beat. |

| CHORDS | Strum: ... | Alternate Strum: ... |

| BASS | Bass line rhythm: ... |

Ramblin'

Grant Gustafson

When two or more notes are played together and the sound is stable and free of tension, the sound is said to be a **CONSONANCE**. When the sound is tense and unstable, it is said to be a **DISSONANCE**.

Most popular music stresses consonance rather than dissonance. However, in order for music to be exciting, it must sometimes contain tension or disturbance. This tension, or dissonance, will usually be resolved into a consonance at some point during the piece.

 Ramblin' Accompaniment

With a partner or with your class, play *Ramblin'* as a duet by combining the melody with the following accompaniment. Notice how the character of the piece is changed. Listen for moments of dissonance as the duet is played. Notice that each time dissonance appears, it is always resolved into consonance. Play this accompaniment in I Position in order to reach the G♯ on the ③ string. Play with the thumb (**p**).

Ramblin'
Accompaniment

Grant Gustafson

Teacher Tips, Student pages 46–47:

- Although students have played exercises in various positions, they have had little experience in changing positions as they play. Explain to students that changing positions to reach notes out of the range of a particular position is known as **shifting**.

- Students are introduced for the first time to playing music without TAB on student page 46. As they progress in their music studies, students will need to become less dependent on TAB. Review the symbols that appear in the music so that students understand what information is provided for them. Remind students that the numbers beside the noteheads are not *frets*, but *finger numbers*. Explain that this is the opposite case with the numbers in the TAB. This will be an important distinction when shifting into II Position, as in the 16th measure of *Cantabile*.

- The first part of *Cantabile* progresses in scale pattern with few large intervals, so a mastery of the A Major scale will be greatly beneficial since TAB is not provided. The second part can be learned by first identifying open strings and fingered notes. Students should be reminded to maintain a steady beat throughout the piece.

Warm-up, Student pages 46–47:

- In order to aid students in being able to play *Cantabile* without TAB, have students master the A Major scale using the in-class scale activities presented on page 52.

Activities, Student pages 46–47:

- Review with students the instructions for reading music with guitar notation in the staff, as opposed to TAB.

- Read to students the discussion of the composer Adam Falckenhagen and the lute provided on student page 46. Further information is provided below.

- Have students complete the *Before You Play* checklist on student page 29 for *Cantabile*. Have students identify passages in *Cantabile* that are the same or similar.

- Rehearse each part of *Cantabile* slowly with students as they become familiar with the guitar fingerings. Then divide the class in half and have students play the duet. When students feel comfortable with this piece, have students perform the piece in pairs before the class.

- Complete the Unit 9 Review checklist with students on student page 47.

Interdisciplinary Studies, Student pages 46–47:

- The lute, a close relative of the guitar, was an important instrument throughout Europe from the 1400s to the 1700s. By the 1500s, the lute had developed into a pear-shaped instrument with six double strings, called courses, and a rounded back. It was played by wandering minstrels and accomplished court musicians. As the lute evolved, strings were added on until it had 13 courses (26 strings) and became too complicated to play and to tune.

  Adam Falckenhagen (1697–1761) composed many works for the solo lute as well as the lute with other instruments, and was one of the great lutenists of the late Baroque period (1600–1750). Music of the Baroque period was distinguished by its complexity, with more than one melody frequently being played at once.

Unit 9 Quiz, Student pages 46–47:

- The duplicable Unit 9 Quiz is provided on page 153. The Unit 9 Quiz tests students on the A Major scale and I, IV, and V7 chords, as well as guitar fingerings, $\frac{5}{4}$ time, consonance, and dissonance.

Guitarists have devised a method of playing from staff notation without the use of tablature:

- A number to the left of a note designates the left hand finger to be used.
- A circled number below a note designates the string to be played. An extended line indicates that all subsequent notes are played on that string.
- A Roman numeral above a note designates the position (no Roman numeral usually means I Position).

Example:

In the example, the note "A" is to be played on the ③ string, with the 2 finger, in I Position.

Cantabile ("singing") was composed by Adam Falckenhagen (1697–1761), a great German lute player and a friend of Johann Sebastian Bach (1685–1750). *Cantabile* was originally written for solo lute. The lute, which was popularized in medieval Europe, is a wooden string instrument similar to the guitar, but pear-shaped. In this arrangement of the work, the melody and bass parts have been separated. Perform the arrangement with a partner or with your class. The lower part (the bass part) should be played with the thumb (**p**) throughout.

Cantabile

Adam Falckenhagen (1697–1761)

Unit 9 Review

Identify:

☐ A Major scale   ☐ consonance

☐ A Major I, IV, V7 chords   ☐ dissonance

☐ $\frac{5}{4}$ time

Perform:

☐ *Ramblin'*

☐ *Ramblin'* Accompaniment

☐ *Cantabile*

Teacher Tips, Student page 48:

• The worksheet format of this page will challenge students to construct a one-octave major scale in the key of E. For students who are less comfortable with music theory, the exercise can be completed together as a class.

• Begin preparing students for the final recital. Arrange the date, time, and place for the final recital. From the songs and compositions students have learned, select those that you would like to have performed. In order to include songs that appear later in the book, concentrate on the appropriate units so that these songs can be learned in time.

Choose pieces that will be challenging for students to prepare, but will also best display students' abilities and technique. Pieces that represent different major and minor as well as different musical expressions should also be chosen. Plan to begin the program with a short, fast-paced song that is both accessible to students and entertaining for the audience. This first song will create a pleasant atmosphere that will help students to become comfortable with giving the recital. Order the pieces in the program so that the audience will remain interested, and close the recital with the students' most impressive work.

Have students practice the songs you have chosen at home, or rehearse them with students at the end of each class period. If desired, coordinate with other instrumental or choir directors to have students from other classes join in the final recital. For example, percussion could be added to *Cielito Lindo* (student pages 50–51), a recorder (playing in unison) on *Pavane* and *Galliard* (student pages 30–31), or a cello (playing in unison) on *El Noy de la Mare* (student page 39).

Warm-up, Student page 48:

• Have students study the G Major, C Major, D Major, and A Major scales to prepare them for completing the E Major scale. If time permits, have students play each one-octave scale twice.

Activities, Student page 48:

• When completing the one-octave E Major scale, have students first fill in the noteheads, write the names of the notes, and then fill in the TAB. Have students then complete the bass tones in the same manner.

• Demonstrate the E, A, and B7 chords for students. The B7 chord is the first chord that demands the use of all four fingers of the left hand. Have students analyze the finger changes between the E chord and the B7 chord and look for the shortest route. (Example: the 2 finger remains in place, the 1 and 3 fingers switch strings, and the 4 finger is added.)

• Complete the *Practicing in E Major* exercise with students.

10 – *BEYOND THE MAJOR BASICS: E MAJOR*

E Major

You have learned the G Major, C Major, D Major, and A Major scales, but there are many more major scales. Using your knowledge of major scales, construct the E Major scale indicated and fill in the E Major bass tones in the worksheet below.

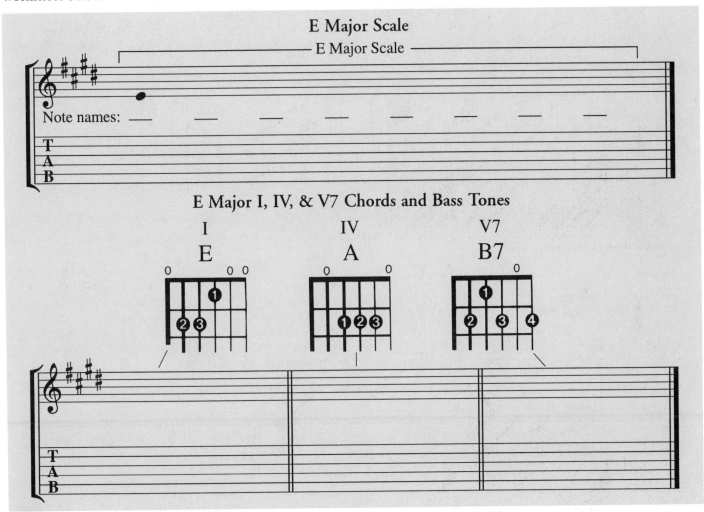

Practicing in E Major

1. Play each note of the E Major scale twice. Practice playing the scale from beginning to end in ascending and descending order, at first slowly and then more quickly.

2. Practice E, A, and B7 chords individually at first, and then as part of a chord progression.

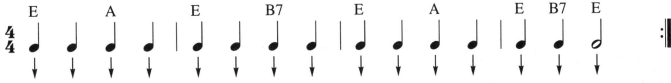

3. Practice the bass tones by playing one bass tone per measure to accompany the chord progression above.

Teacher Tips, Student page 49:

• In rock music, power chords are generally played with a pick or plectrum. On the nylon string acoustic guitar, either a very soft plectrum or the back of the fingernail of the **m** or **i** finger may be used.

• The "5" behind the power chord letter name signifies that the chord structure includes the root and the fifth. The defining major or minor third is missing. Students will gain a better understanding of the structure of major and minor chords by studying Worksheet 6, correlated with student page 53 (page 143). The structure of a power chord can be explained in conjunction with this worksheet.

• *Power Jam* is a study in E Major that exercises the ascending and descending E Major scale.

• Chord charts are provided for E5, B5, and A5 below. The B5 and A5 charts show an alternate position used by many guitarists. Rather than changing strings, all three of the power chords can be played on the ⑥ and ⑤ strings. The root of the chord is the tone on the ⑥ string.

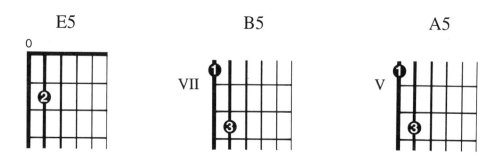

Activities, Student page 49:

• Students should prepare the power chords in *Power Jam Accompaniment* by leaving the 2 finger on the ④ string, 2nd fret (E) throughout. Rehearse *Power Jam Accompaniment* with the class.

• Have students practice *Power Jam* as a class. Once students have mastered *Power Jam*, divide the class in two groups and have one group accompany the other with the power chords.

• Ask students if they know songs that make use of power chords. Play some examples in class and have students identify where the power chords are being played.

• For more advanced students, have them figure out the power chords for other chords they have learned in the book using E5, B5, and A5 in the key of E Major as examples. Then have students accompany each other on songs using the power chords.

Power chords are two-note chords played on the lower strings of the guitar, and are indicated with a 5 after the letter. They create a hard-driving rhythm and are often found in rock music.

 Power Jam Accompaniment

To play the power chords below, strike both strings in a downward motion, playing the root of the power chord first.

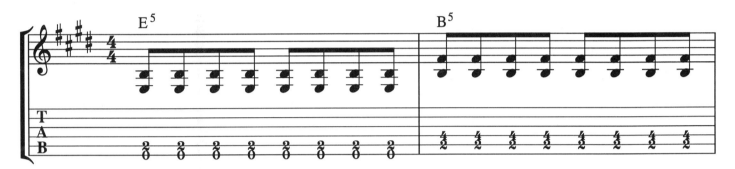

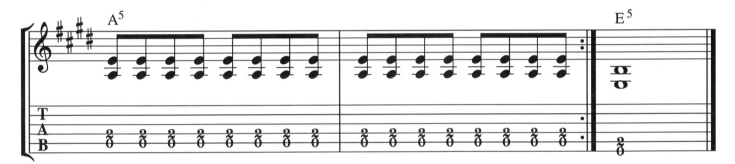

 Power Jam

MELODY	The 4th and 8th measures are E Major scale patterns in descending and ascending order.
CHORDS	Play the above accompaniment, repeating it four times.
BASS	Play one bass tone on the first beat of each measure.

Power Jam

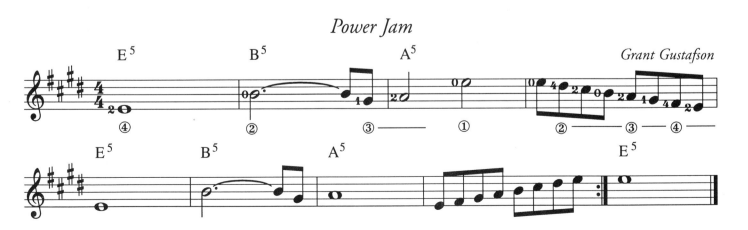

Grant Gustafson

Teacher Tips, Student pages 50–51:

• Syncopations in various forms will be introduced throughout the remainder of this book. Students should understand the underlying principle that an accent is transferred from a weak beat to a strong beat.

• In the folk music of middle and south America, the guitar is often used as a percussion instrument. This ranges from tapping the soundboard and sides to slapping the strings against the frets. These percussions are integrated into the accompaniment and interact with chord strums. As in *El Noy de la Mare* on student page 39, the chord strum pattern for *Cielito Lindo* includes a slap against the strings.

• The guitar can also be used in other percussive ways to accompany this song. It can be turned into a bongo by playing the back side of the guitar. Cow bells can be imitated by crossing the ① and ② strings at the 7th fret.

• Percussion instruments can also be added to accompany this song, such as maracas and marimbas.

• The lyrics to *Cielito Lindo* in the original Spanish have been included in order to reinforce the word-rhythm association. Some students may already be familiar with the song and the words. For those who are not, learning the words to a song in an unfamiliar language will help develop their appreciation for other cultures. The words can also be used as an opportunity to work with a Spanish class in learning this song.

Activities, Student pages 50–51:

• Review with students the definition of **syncopation** provided on student page 50.

• To prepare for playing *Syncopation*, first have the entire class clap quarter notes in ¾ time, with emphasis placed on the first beat of each measure. Then, divide the class into two sections. The first section continues to clap quarter notes while the second section claps the rhythm of the *Syncopation* exercise. When the note is tied over from the strong first beat, the emphasis should be placed on the third beat of the measure preceding it.

• The music of middle and south America combine these syncopations to create polyrhythms (multiple rhythms). The polyrhythm that results from the exercise above, is:

This rhythm appears in *Cielito Lindo* when the bass tone plays on the first beat of each measure while the melody plays the syncopations:

• Once students have mastered clapping the rhythms, have them play *Syncopation* on their instruments.

- Review the chord strum pattern for *Cielito Lindo*. This is the same slapping noise in the chord strum pattern for *El Noy de la Mare* on student page 39. Let students experiment by placing the slap on different beats.

- Rehearse the melody of *Cielito Lindo* with students. Once students have mastered the melody, divide the class into three groups and assign each group a part.

- Explain to students that "Cielito Lindo" means "beautiful little heaven." The words to the song describe how happy singing can make us.

- To create harmonic interest, write out a second melody part in intervals of thirds or sixths to the song melody on the duplicable blank staff/TAB provided on page 158. Divide the class so that some students can play the main melody, and others can play the second melody.

- After students have mastered *Cielito Lindo*, duplicate and distribute the Evaluation Worksheet on page 159. Divide students into groups of five. Ask each student to perform the one-octave E Major scale, the E Major chord progression (student page 48), and the melody of *Cielito Lindo*. Have the other students in the group evaluate the performer based on the criteria provided on the worksheet.

- Complete the Unit 10 Review checklist with students.

Interdisciplinary Studies, Student pages 50–51:

- Read the following cultural background for *Cielito Lindo* to students:

Cielito Lindo is a traditional folk song from Mexico. Mexico is the largest country in Central America, and lies directly south of the United States. Mexico City is the capital of Mexico.

The music and dance of Mexico is very distinctive. One of the most popular types of Mexican music is mariachi music. Violins and trumpets play the melody while a guitar provides an accompaniment and a *guitarron* (a large Mexican guitar) plays the bass line. The performers often sing humorous lyrics along with the music. Mariachi music is often performed in the colorful plazas, or town squares, of Mexican cities.

Unit 10 Quiz, Student pages 50–51:

- The duplicable Unit 10 Quiz is provided on page 154. The Unit 10 Quiz tests students on all five one-octave major scales that they have learned and on syncopation.

When the rhythm of the music places an accent in a measure on a naturally unaccented, or weak, beat, an effect known as **SYNCOPATION** is created. Often, syncopation is created with ties or long note values extending into a strong beat.

Syncopation

Practice clapping the syncopated rhythm below, counting as you clap. Then play the rhythms with your class.

Cielito Lindo

MELODY

The syncopation exercise above will prepare you to play the rhythms in *Cielito Lindo*. Listen carefully to the chords and bass tones to stay in time.

CHORDS

Strum:

* Slap the strings against the fingerboard with the fingers to create a percussive sound.

BASS

Bass line rhythm:

Cielito Lindo

Mexican Folk Song

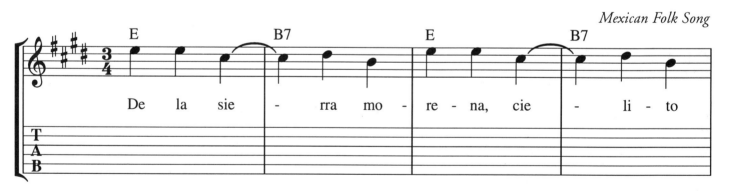

De la sie - rra mo - re - na, cie - li - to

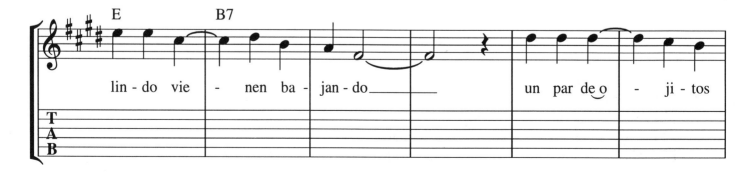

lin - do vie - nen ba - jan - do_____ un par de o - ji - tos

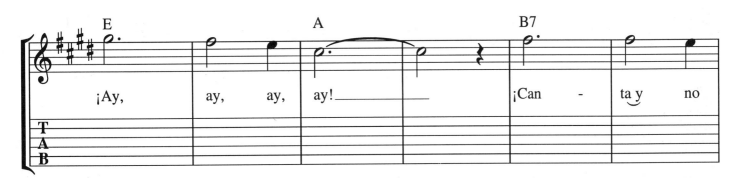

Unit 10 Review

Identify:

- ☐ E Major scale
- ☐ E Major I, IV, V7 chords
- ☐ power chords
- ☐ syncopation

Perform:

- ☐ *Power Jam*
- ☐ *Cielito Lindo*

Teacher Tips, Student pages 52–53:

• Students have now mastered the sounds and fingerings of several major keys. Students should be able to see and hear the differences between major and minor scales by studying the pattern of half and whole steps in the A Minor scales on student page 52.

• Explain to students that the interval between the first and third notes of a major scale is a **major third** (two whole steps) and the interval between the first and third notes of a minor scale is a **minor third** (one whole step and one half step).

• For more advanced students, explain that a major key which shares the same key signature as a minor key is called a **relative key**. Chords are often interchangeable between these relative keys.

• Have students concentrate on learning the A Natural Minor scale on student page 53, but also introduce the A Harmonic and A Melodic Minor scales. Students should understand that the sixth and seventh notes of the minor scale frequently change within a song.

• The A Minor scales on student page 53 can be played in I Position, with a position change to reach the last note, A, at the fifth fret. The shift in the A Natural Minor scale is indicated with an asterix. The A Harmonic Minor scale and the ascending A Melodic Minor scale are written in staff notation and the recommended shift is indicated by a "II." above the note. Remind students, while changing positions, to remain relaxed, leaving the thumb in place beneath the neck, and letting the arm "fall" into the new position.

• Students may ask why the i and iv chords are represented by lowercase letters. Explain to students that the i and iv chords are minor chords, while the dominant seventh chord, V7, is always a major chord. Refer to Worksheet 6, page 143.

Activities, Student pages 52–53:

• Review the definitions of **minor scale**, **natural minor scale**, **harmonic minor scale**, and **melodic minor scale** and the examples provided on student page 52. Play each example scale for students so they can hear the difference.

• After students have played the first five notes of the A Major and A Minor scales in the *Major and Minor Scales* exercise on student page 52, play the first five notes of another major and minor scale, such as E Major and E Minor, and have students identify which scales have been played.

• Play familiar songs in major, then play them for students in a minor key. Have students identify which note is the third note of the scale.

• Play through each of the A Minor scales on student page 53 with students, and demonstrate the A min, D min, and E7 chords. Have students choose a rhythmic pattern for playing the A Minor chord progression, and rehearse it with the class. Then, have students play the bass tones indicated using the same chord progression.

• Give students an ear training quiz by playing the three different A Minor scales and the A Major scale, and asking students to identify each scale.

Worksheet 6, Student pages 52–53:

• The duplicable Worksheet 6 is provided on page 143. Worksheet 6 provides an overview of major and minor chord structure. Review the information in class, or have students read the worksheet as a homework assignment.

11– A Change of Mood: A Minor

A **MINOR SCALE** is an eight-note scale which uses each note of the music alphabet. Minor scales sound different from major scales because they follow different patterns of half steps and whole steps. There are three types of minor scales.

The **NATURAL MINOR SCALE** has half steps between the second and third, and fifth and sixth notes of the scale.

A Natural Minor Scale

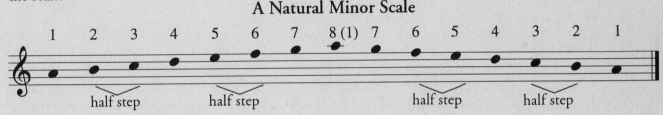

The **HARMONIC MINOR SCALE** is different from the natural minor scale in that the 7th note is raised a half step.

A Harmonic Minor Scale

The **MELODIC MINOR SCALE** raises both the 6th and 7th notes of the natural minor scale when the scale is ascending. When the scale is descending, the notes are the same as the natural minor scale.

A Melodic Minor Scale

Major and Minor Scales

Study the first five tones of the A Major scale and the A Minor scale, shown below. Notice that the two scales are the same except for the third tone in the scale. The third tone of the major scale is a half step higher than the third tone of the minor scale. Mark the intervals between the notes as "half" or "whole" on each scale. Then play each example, and listen for the difference.

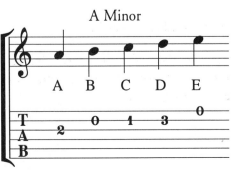

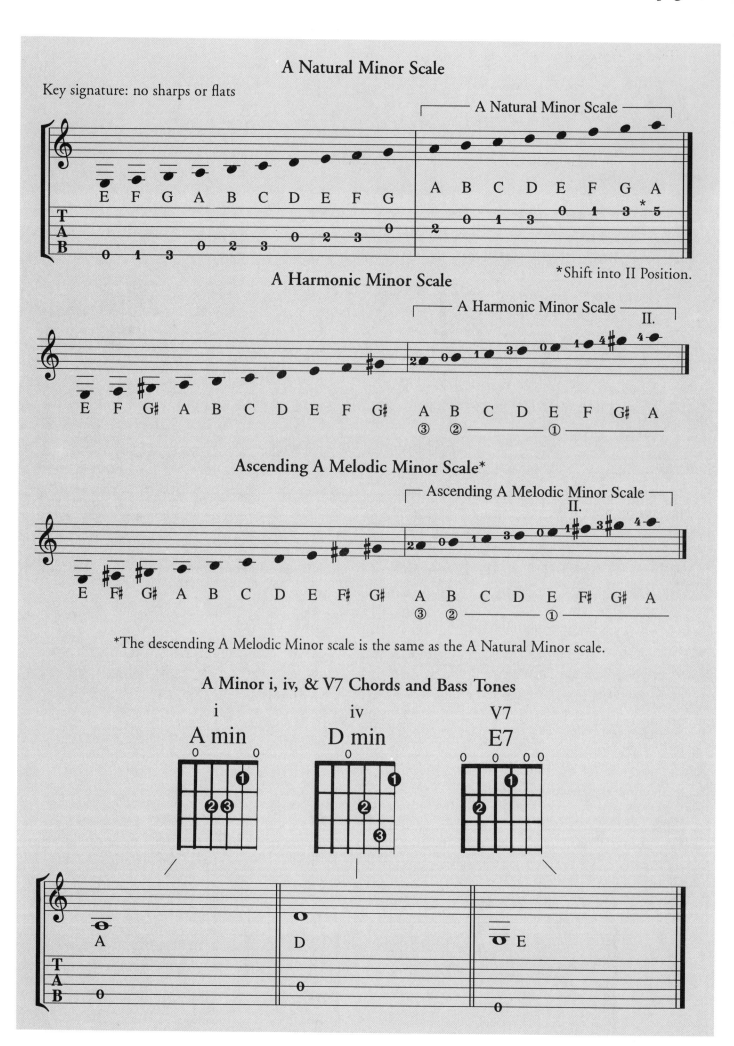

A Natural Minor Scale

Key signature: no sharps or flats

A Natural Minor Scale

*Shift into II Position.

A Harmonic Minor Scale

A Harmonic Minor Scale

Ascending A Melodic Minor Scale*

Ascending A Melodic Minor Scale

*The descending A Melodic Minor scale is the same as the A Natural Minor scale.

A Minor i, iv, & V7 Chords and Bass Tones

i — A min

iv — D min

V7 — E7

Teacher Tips, Student pages 54–55:

• *Greensleeves* is a well-known song which will introduce students to playing a song in a minor key.

• C and G Major chords appear in this arrangement of *Greensleeves*, even though the song is in A Minor. Refer students back to student page 27 to remind them how to play these major chords.

• In the 14th full measure, students should be reminded to leave the 1 finger on the G♯ while extending the 4 finger to play F♯.

Activities, Student pages 54–55:

• Have students fill in the TAB if they wish. Rehearse the melody of *Greensleeves* with students. Once they have mastered the melody, divide the class into three groups and assign each group a part.

• Have students sing while they play once they are familiar with the song.

• Ask more advanced students to identify the melodic and harmonic minor scale variations in *Greensleeves*.

• After students have mastered *Greensleeves*, duplicate and distribute the Evaluation Worksheet on page 159. Divide students into groups of five. Ask each student to perform the one-octave A Natural Minor scale, an A Minor chord progression of the student's choice, and the melody of *Greensleeves*. Have the other students in the group evaluate the performer based on the criteria provided on the worksheet. This activity could be alternatively completed after students have mastered *The Birch Tree* (student page 56).

Interdisciplinary Studies, Student pages 54–55:

• Read the following cultural background of *Greensleeves* to students:

Greensleeves is a song originating in England. England is part of the United Kingdom of Great Britain and Northern Ireland. The island nation lies northwest of France. London is the capital of the United Kingdom.

Greensleeves was particularly popular in England in the late 1500s, and was even mentioned in a play by the famous English author William Shakespeare (1564–1616). At that time, *Greensleeves* was a fast-paced dance tune, but through the ages it has become a slower song like a ballad.

Greensleeves

MELODY

Be sure to connect the notes to create smooth phrasing. In the 14th and 30th full measures, leave the 1st finger on the 1st fret while stretching with the 4th finger to play F♯ on the ④ string.

CHORDS

Although *Greensleeves* is in the key of A Minor, C and G chords appear. Chords can function and progress in many ways. As you continue your musical studies, you will learn more about chord progressions such as the one in *Greensleeves*. Play the C and G chords with the fingerings you have already learned.

Strum:

BASS

Play the C and G bass tones which you have already learned, in addition to the A Minor bass tones.

Bass line rhythm:

Greensleeves

English Folk Song (16th century)

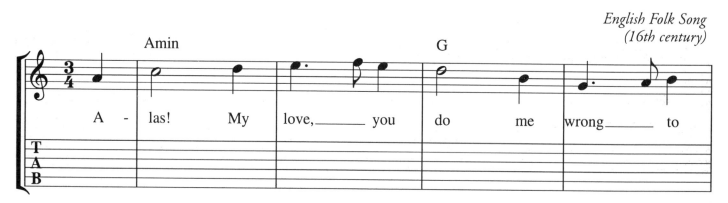

Amin   G

A - las!   My   love,_____ you   do   me   wrong_____ to

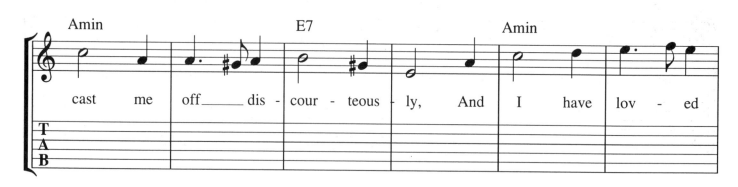

Amin   E7   Amin

cast   me   off_____ dis - cour - teous - ly,   And   I   have   lov - ed

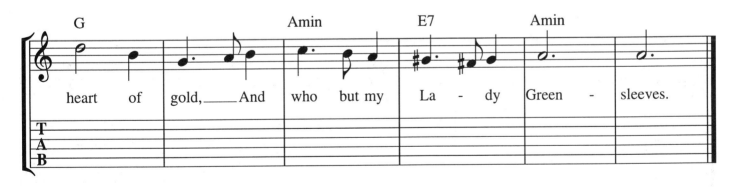

Teacher Tip, Student page 56:

• *The Birch Tree* is in staff notation, with guitar fingerings to better locate the notes. For students who have difficulty playing without TAB, explain that staff notation is advantageous because it presents not only the note but the duration of the note.

Warm-up, Student page 56:

• Have students play the A Natural Minor scale to prepare them for playing a tune without TAB.

Activities, Student page 56:

• Have students complete the *Before You Play* checklist (student page 29) for *The Birch Tree*. This will help them to become familiar with the music so that playing without TAB is not as difficult.

• Practice the chord strum pattern and bass line rhythm with students.

• Rehearse the melody of *The Birch Tree* with students. Once students have mastered the melody, divide the class into three groups and assign each group a part.

• Complete the Unit 11 Review with students.

• Explain to students that Russian composer Peter Ilyich Tchaikovsky (1840–1893) used *The Birch Tree* as the basis for the main theme of the Finale of his Symphony No. 4. If you have a recording, share with students excerpts of Tchaikovsky's Symphony No. 4 where *The Birch Tree* melody appears. Ask students to comment on the differences between the sound of Tchaikovsky's arrangement and the three-part arrangement of the song provided on student page 56.

Interdisciplinary Studies, Student page 56:

• Read the following cultural background of *The Birch Tree* to students:

The Birch Tree is a folk tune from Russia, a country in eastern Europe and Asia, which in physical size is the largest country in the world. Since 1991, Russia has been an independent republic, with Moscow as its capital.

Ballet, opera, literature, music, and art have long been an essential part of Russian life. In Moscow today, there are some 80 museums dedicated to the great artistic treasures of Russia. Russian ballet and opera troupes continue to tour outside of Russia, receiving widespread admiration.

Russian folk music is a vast subject, and many Russian composers incorporated folk tunes into their music. Peter Ilyich Tchaikovsky (1840–1893), for example, based the theme of the fourth movement of his Symphony No. 4 on *The Birch Tree*. The beautiful melody of *The Birch Tree* becomes a dramatic, fast-paced tune, typical of Tchaikovsky's passionate, complex style.

Unit 11 Quiz, Student page 56:

• The duplicable Unit 11 Quiz is provided on page 155. The Unit 11 Quiz asks students to identify the A Major, A Natural Minor, A Harmonic Minor, and ascending A Melodic Minor scales, the i, iv, and V7 chords of A Minor, as well as the guitar fingerings for notes in the one-octave A Natural Minor scale.

As you become more comfortable with scale patterns and notes, you will begin to rely less on tablature. Therefore, for the remainder of the book, tablature will become less and less frequent.

 The Birch Tree

| MELODY | When playing without TAB, master the scale in which a piece is composed, then identify the highest and lowest notes as well as repetitive rhythmic patterns. In this melody, the tune flows in scale progression with very few jumps. |

| CHORDS | Strum: 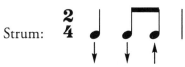 |

| BASS | Play one bass tone on each chord change. In the 4th measure, play an A on beat 1, since the A Minor chord continues from the previous measure. |

The Birch Tree

Russian Folk Song

Unit 11 Review

Identify:

☐ minor scale   ☐ melodic minor scale   Perform:
☐ natural minor scale   ☐ A Minor scales   ☐ *Greensleeves*
☐ harmonic minor scale   ☐ A Minor i, iv, V7 chords   ☐ *The Birch Tree*

Teacher Tip, Student page 57:

• In preparation for the final recital, finalize arrangements for the date, time, and place of the recital. Be sure students know which pieces will be included so that they can be practicing at home. If additional instruments will be included, choose instrumentalists for these parts. Be sure to schedule rehearsal times for all of your guitar classes to meet in a "guitar orchestra" prior to the final recital.

Students may enjoy preparing short program notes to be presented to the audience before each piece. Ask for volunteers who would like to prepare program notes for each piece, such as the historical or cultural background of the work, a biographical note on the composer, a description of rhythmic or melodic elements, or a demonstration of a special guitar technique that will appear in the work.

Activities, Student page 57:

• Play each of the E Minor scales with students, playing each tone of the scale twice. Have students identify the half steps in each scale.

• Demonstrate the E min, A min, and B7 chords for students, and have them strum the chords along with you. Point out to students that they have already learned the A min chord on student page 53.

• Have students choose a rhythmic pattern to use for practicing the chord progression. Write the chord progression and rhythm on the board, and rehearse it with students. Then, have students play the bass tones indicated using the same chord progression.

• Ask students to compare and contrast the E Natural Minor scale with the E Major scale, on student page 48.

12 – A CHANGE OF MOOD: E MINOR

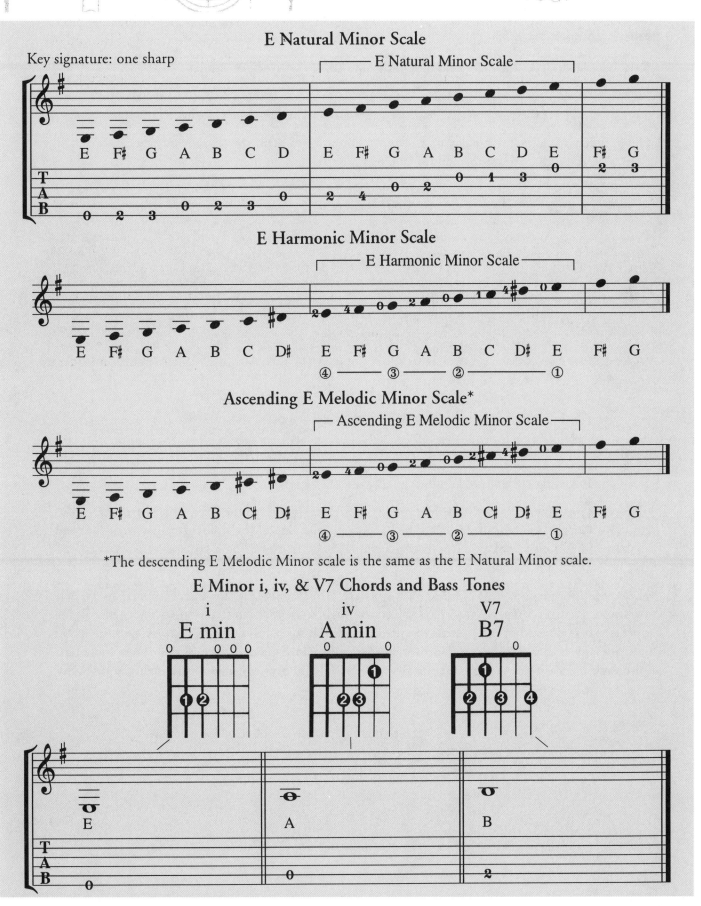

Teacher Tip, Student page 58:

- Triplets pose a special challenge to the musician, as they are difficult to subdivide into smaller units. Students may benefit from practicing triplet clapping exercises over the span of a few class periods.

Activities, Student page 58:

- Review with students the definition of **eighth note triplet** provided on student page 58.

- Divide the class into two groups. Have one group clap steady quarter notes. Once they have attained a steady beat, have the other group clap three times for each quarter note clap. Switch roles and repeat.

- Have students analyze the melody of *Habanera*. Point out to them that the melody descends in half steps. Ask them to consider the emotional effect that this has on the melody.

- Remind students of the meaning of sharps, flats, and naturals that appear within music. Review the fingerings for C♯ and D♯ on the ② string if students are having difficulties.

- Practice the chord strum with students. Rehearse both the melody and the bass line with students. When they have mastered both parts, divide the class into two groups and assign each group a part. Switch roles and repeat.

- Arrange further sections of the "Habanera" for students from Georges Bizet's *Carmen* in the same manner to extend this into a concert-performance piece.

- If you have a recording of "Habanera" from the opera *Carmen* by Georges Bizet, share it with students.

Interdisciplinary Studies, Student page 58:

- Read the following cultural background for *Habanera* to students:

The name "habanera" comes from Havanna, Cuba. The rhythm of the habanera, like much of the music of Cuba, is of African descent. The habanera is also one of the influences that went into the making of the "tango," which is closely associated with this rhythm. The habanera's popularity spread to Europe, and especially to Spain.

Habanera on student page 58 is based on the melody from a song from the opera *Carmen*, by French composer Georges Bizet (1838–1875). Bizet was highly talented, and composed many important operas that premiered in Paris during his life. One of his most famous operas, *Carmen*, tells the tragic life story of a young gypsy woman of Spain, and the "Habanera" is one of the songs she sings. Although the Parisians thought the opera was too bold and exotic, *Carmen's* originality and vitality make it well-loved today.

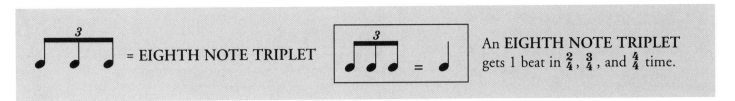

= EIGHTH NOTE TRIPLET

An **EIGHTH NOTE TRIPLET** gets 1 beat in $\frac{2}{4}$, $\frac{3}{4}$, and $\frac{4}{4}$ time.

 Habanera (from the opera *Carmen*)

MELODY — Listen to the effect created by the melody which descends in half steps. Distribute the eighth notes in each triplet evenly over the space of one beat.

CHORDS — The chord symbols are written between the melody and bass lines.

Strum:

BASS — The bass line is provided on the second staff line.

Habanera

Georges Bizet (1838–1875)

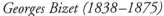

Teacher Tips, Student page 59:

• *Count and Clap* and *Syncopated Sixteenths* have been included to prepare the students for the syncopations found in *To Get Back*, student pages 60–61.

• *Syncopated Sixteenths* is played only on the open ③ string. The syncopations occur in the last two measures of each line. Remind students that in a syncopation, the accent is transferred from a weak beat to a strong beat.

• It is essential for students to listen to the clapping when playing these exercises. The clapping section should be steady and maintain the beat.

Activities, Student page 59:

• Review with students the definition of **eighth/sixteenth note combination** provided on student page 59.

• Have students write in the counting for *Count and Clap*. Then have students practice clapping each line before dividing the class into two groups to play the exercise as a duet.

• Review the definition of syncopation provided on student page 50.

• Play the top line of *Syncopated Sixteenths* for students and have them identify in which measure(s) there are syncopated rhythms. Then divide the class into two groups, and assign a part to each group. Switch roles and repeat the exercise.

• Play recordings of popular or other music, and ask students to identify syncopated rhythms.

= EIGHTH/SIXTEENTH NOTE COMBINATIONS

Count and Clap

In the exercise below, write the counting. The counting for the first measure has been completed for you. As you play, count sixteenth notes aloud, carefully observing the right hand fingering indications. Perform the exercise while others clap the rhythm shown.

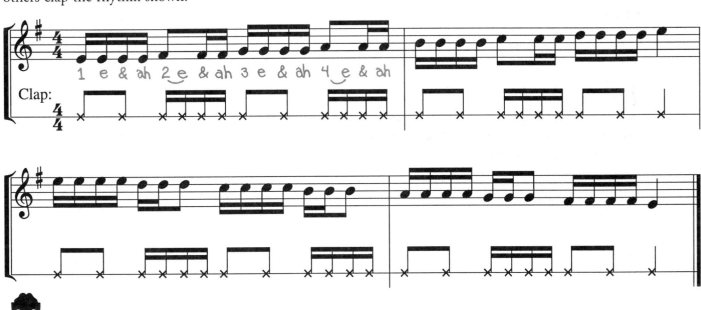

Syncopated Sixteenths

As you play the syncopated rhythm below, count sixteenth notes aloud. Perform the exercise while others clap the rhythm indicated.

Teacher Tips, Student pages 60–61:

- Student pages 60–61 are provided on pages 118–119.

- Measures 1–4 of *To Get Back* should be played "as if spoken." The chords should be strummed with a downstroke only once at each point where a chord symbol is provided. One bass tone should also be played at each chord change.

- For measures 5–48 of *To Get Back*, the chord strum pattern provided on student page 60 should be used. The bass should play the bass line given on student book page 60 during the chord progression G – C – Emin – C, as indicated. In measures 21–26 and 35–47, when the chord progression varies, students should play one bass tone at each chord change.

Warm-up, Student pages 60–61:

- Have students play *Syncopated Sixteenths* on student page 59 to prepare for the rhythms in *To Get Back*.

Activities, Student pages 60–61:

- Review the instructions for playing chords and bass tones for *To Get Back*. Rehearse the bass line with students.

- Rehearse the melody of *To Get Back* with students. Since the rhythms in *To Get Back* are more difficult than in previous songs, students may need to practice counting or clapping the melody together in order to master the rhythms.

- Once students have mastered the melody of *To Get Back*, divide the class into two groups, and have one group play the melody while the other plays the chords. Switch roles and repeat. Complete the same activity with the bass line instead of the chords. Once students feel comfortable with each of the parts, divide the class into three groups and assign each group a part.

- *To Get Back* can be performed in the following arrangements:

As an instrumental ensemble piece without using the lyrics.

As an instrumental ensemble/vocal piece with a vocal ensemble.

As an instrumental ensemble piece with a solo vocalist.

One guitarist on chords, one guitarist on bass, and a solo vocalist.

One vocalist-guitarist performing the melody and words.

One guitarist combining the chords and bass, with a solo vocalist.

The above arrangement possibilities can be used for most of the songs in this book.

- For more advanced students, the question may be asked why the major chords G and C fit so well in a song in the key of E Minor. Students may be aided by an explanation of the concept of **relative keys**: a major key and a minor key which have the same key signature. Since E Minor and G Major are relative keys, composers will sometimes add G Major chords to E Minor tunes. Have students identify the relative key of A Minor.

Teacher Tips, Student pages 62–63:

- Student pages 62–63 are provided on pages 120–121.

- Left hand fingerings are not provided in this piece. Students may fill in the fingerings as they feel necessary.

- Note how the rhythm in all three parts is very similar. In essence, the guitar ensemble is playing chords in the same rhythm.

Activities, Student pages 62–63:

- Review with students the information about King Henry VIII provided on student page 62. Further information is provided below.

- Practice counting and clapping the dotted quarter/eighth note combination and the dotted eighth/sixteenth note combination to prepare students for the rhythms in this piece.

- Rehearse each part with students. Remind students to play with the thumb when playing part C, the bass line. Once students have mastered each part, divide the class into three groups and have each group play a part.

- Students will enjoy changing this composition into a more modern work. A steady, raucous strum of the chords, while the melody is playing, will transport this composition into modern rock. Use the following chord strum pattern and play the chords indicated.

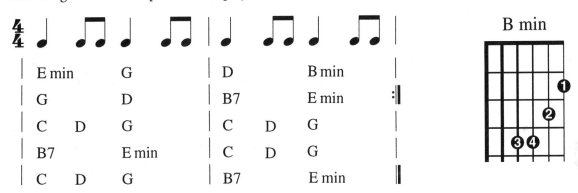

E min		G		D		B min
G		D		B7		E min
C	D	G		C	D	G
B7		E min		C	D	G
C	D	G		B7		E min

B min

- Other instruments, such as flutes, bassoons, and violins or drums, electric bass, and electric guitars can be added to accompany this piece.

- Complete the Unit 12 Review checklist with students.

Interdisciplinary Studies, Student pages 62–63:

- Read the following historical background for *Pastime with Good Company* to students:

Henry VIII of England (1491–1547) was a popular, outgoing man with a passion for hunting, music, and the arts. He had many artist friends, one of whom painted several portraits of the King which are still famous today. Henry VIII's interests fit the mood of the Renaissance period (1400–1600), in which he lived, when parties, dancing, music, and art were growing in importance. However, he is perhaps best remembered for his aggressive military policy against France and Scotland and his six wives. He had three children who all later ruled England: Edward VI, Mary I, and Elizabeth I.

Unit 12 Quiz, Student pages 62–63:

- The duplicable Unit 12 Quiz is provided on page 156. The Unit 12 Quiz asks students to identify the E Major, E Natural Minor, E Harmonic Minor, and ascending E Melodic Minor scale and the i, iv, and V7 chords of the E Minor scale. Students are also tested on triplets and eighth/sixteenth note combinations.

To Get Back

| MELODY | Throughout *To Get Back*, count the eighth/sixteenth note combinations and the syncopated rhythms carefully. |

| CHORDS | In measures 1–4, strum once each time a chord symbol appears. |

Strum in measures 5–48: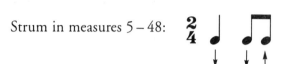

Although *To Get Back* is in the key of E Minor, C and G chords appear. Play the C and G chords with the fingerings you have already learned.

| BASS | Play one bass tone at each chord change in measures 1–4, 21–26, and 35–47. Play the following bass line in measures 5–20 and measures 27–34 along with the G C E min C chord progression: |

Otherwise, play the bass tones of the chords in half notes.

To Get Back

Lory Ann Darnell

In addition to ruling England for 38 years, King Henry VIII (1491–1547) was an accomplished musician and a friend of many artists and scholars. Besides these interests, he enjoyed parties, sports, and hunting. *Pastime with Good Company* was a popular song composed by King Henry VIII.

Pastime with Good Company

The rhythm ♩. ♪ appears in most measures of this piece. Wait to play the eighth note until after you have counted and felt the beat that precedes it. Although this song does not have fingerings or strings notated, you should be able to play these notes. The C part should be played with the thumb (**p**) throughout.

Pastime with Good Company

King Henry VIII of England

Unit 12 Review

Identify:
☐ E Minor scales
☐ E Minor i, iv, V7 chords
☐ eight note triplet

☐ eighth/sixteenth
   note combinations

Perform:
☐ *Habanera*
☐ *To Get Back*
☐ *Pastime with Good Company*

Teacher Tips, Student page 64:

- The activities and exercises throughout this book have encouraged creativity and ingenuity from the beginning. Learning to improvise will further build on students' ability to be creative with music.

- Remind students that music is like language: the more vocabulary you master, the better you are able to express yourself. Learning scale and chord patterns is as important as learning grammatical sentence structures.

- The pentatonic scale in E Minor is an effective scale for learning to improvise melodies. Since there are no half steps (no dissonances), it sounds consonant no matter how it is played. It is like playing only the black keys on the piano.

- For more advanced students, discuss what makes the E Minor Pentatonic scale "minor." An E Major Pentatonic scale would be constructed differently: E F♯ G♯ B C♯ E.

Activities, Student page 64:

- Review with students the definitions of **pentatonic scale** and **improvisation** provided on student page 64.

- Play the E Minor Pentatonic scale with students, repeating each note twice.

- Divide the class into pairs, and have students select an aphorism discussed on student page 9 and play it using tones from the E Minor Pentatonic scale.

- Divide the class into pairs, and have students select a rhythmic pattern and play tones from the E Minor Pentatonic scale to this rhythm.

- Divide the class into pairs, and have students do the dialogue exercises described on page 12, but using tones from the E Minor Pentatonic scale rather than percussive noises.

- Create a bass riff and teach it to the class. Have students play it softly while one student improvises on the E Minor Pentatonic scale. Example:

- Play the 12-bar blues chord progression in E Major while students improvise on the E Minor Pentatonic scale.

- Review the instructions for *Improvising with the Pentatonic Scale* with students. Have students complete the activity at home or in class, and ask volunteers to play their compositions for the class.

13–THE PENTATONIC SCALE

A **PENTATONIC SCALE** is any scale made up of five notes. Usually, the five notes divide the octave fairly evenly, with no single large interval. There are many different forms of the pentatonic scale, and one of them is shown below.

E Minor Pentatonic Scale

IMPROVISATION is the art of creating music as you perform. Since scales and chords are the building blocks of music, learning as many scales and chord progressions as possible will help improvisation skills. But, you can also improvise with just a couple of notes by playing them in various orders and rhythms. It helps to remember that music is communication. When you improvise, imagine that you are expressing a particular message in musical code to another person or to an audience.

 ## Improvising with the Pentatonic Scale

As with language, music needs to have a structure to be understood. The organization of rhythm and pitch helps give music this structure. When improvising, rhythms and pitches should be organized in such a way that the intended message is communicated. Expressing an understandable message in music requires the use of rhythm and pitch patterns (scales), regardless of whether this message is written down or improvised.

With this in mind, improvise a melody (musical message) by playing the pitches from the E Minor Pentatonic scale, using the rhythm below. Experiment with the order in which you play the notes of the scale. Then, write your favorite on the blank staff.

Teacher Tip, Student page 65:

• The melody of *The Wind* uses the tones of the E Minor Pentatonic scale.

Activities, Student page 65:

• Read to students the information on pentatonic scales provided on student page 65.

• Have students clap the rhythm in *Eighth Note Syncopations* together. Ask students to identify in which measure(s) syncopated rhythms appear, and where the stress is felt. Then, have students play the exercise on their instruments.

• Demonstrate the E5 power chord for students, and have them strum the chord along with you.

• Ask students to observe how short, different rhythmic units are repeated, combined, and turned around to create unity and variety in this composition. Have students identify the different rhythmic units.

• Rehearse the melody of *The Wind* with students. If students are having difficulty with the syncopation in the 11th and 13th measures, have half of the students clap steady eighth notes while others play the melody. Once students have mastered the melody, divide the class into two groups and have one group play the melody while the other group plays the E5 power chords.

• More advanced students may be encouraged to create a composition of their own in the style of *The Wind*, by using tones from the E Minor Pentatonic scale and short, concise rhythmic units.

• Complete the Unit 13 Review checklist.

Interdisciplinary Studies, Student page 65:

• Read the following cultural background for *The Wind* to students:

The Wind is a folk song native to China. A vast country in eastern Asia, China has the largest population of any country in the world — about 1 billion. The capital of China is Beijing. Hong Kong, long governed by Great Britain, returned to Chinese rule in 1997.

China is famous the world over for its artwork. Jade and ivory carvings, delicate paintings on silk scrolls, and lustrous vases of the Ming period are all admired.

Opera is one important aspect of the Chinese musical tradition. The stories for Chinese opera come from historical epics, folk legends, and fairy tales. The performers wear beautiful costumes and fascinating make-up. Musical instruments include gongs, drums, Chinese fiddles, flutes, wooden clappers, and cymbals.

The pentatonic scale is used in contemporary art music as well as in the folk music of many cultures of the world, including Japan, China, and Native America.

Eighth Note Syncopations

Practice clapping the syncopated rhythm below, counting as you clap. Then play the rhythms with your class.

The Wind

MELODY   The syncopation exercise above will prepare you to play the rhythms in *The Wind*. The E Minor Pentatonic scale provides the tones for this piece.

CHORDS   Create a gong effect by playing the E5 power chord on the first beat of each measure:

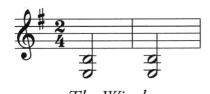

The Wind

Chinese Folk Song

Unit 13 Review

Identify:
- ☐ pentatonic scale
- ☐ E Minor Pentatonic Scale
- ☐ improvisation

Perform:
- ☐ *The Wind*

Teacher Tip, Student page 66:

• The 12-bar blues form is the basis for much jazz and rock, and is accessible to students.

Activities, Student page 66:

• Review with students the definitions of **blues**, **blues scale**, and 12-bar blues form.

• Play the E Blues scale with students, repeating each note twice. The E Blues scale has been provided in two octaves to provide students with a wider range when improvising.

• Play recordings of the blues in different styles so that the students hear the 12-bar blues form. Examples: Muddy Waters, W.C. Handy, B.B. King, Elvis Presley, The Beatles, The Rolling Stones, Jimi Hendrix, Eric Clapton, Led Zeppelin. Ask students to describe what they feel the blues expresses.

• Review with students the instructions for *Playing the Blues*. Have students complete each step of the activity, perhaps over several class periods. Prepare sample **riffs** to play for the class to give them ideas for steps 2 and 3.

• Have students improvise on the 12-bar blues form in the key of E, using the E Minor Pentatonic scale.

• Have students work in pairs to compose their own lyrics for the 12-bar blues form and set the lyrics to music. Have volunteers perform their compositions for the class.

Interdisciplinary Studies, Student page 66:

• Read the following historical background for the blues to students:

The blues, which originated in the rural southern United States, had spread to the saloons and theaters of American cities by the 1920s and 1930s. African-American women like Ma Rainey (1886–1939) and Bessie Smith (1894–1937) sang about their anxieties, misfortunes, and dreams, while a band consisting of a trumpet, trombone, saxophone, guitar, and piano accompanied. The blues offered instrumentalists the opportunity to improvise and to experiment with sounds. This inventive style of music was to be one of the sources of jazz and rock music.

Worksheet 7, Student page 66:

• The duplicable Worksheet 7 is provided on page 144. Worksheet 7 provides students with the opportunity to compose a 12-bar blues composition.

14—THE BLUES

The **BLUES** is a musical style which developed in the United States in the early 20th century, based upon African-American spirituals and work songs of the rural southern United States. The **BLUES SCALE** captures the mood of the blues. The notes of the blues scale are the basis of many blues melodies and can be used in blues improvisation. The E Blues scale below is related to the E Minor Pentatonic Scale, but includes A♯, which is called a "blue note."

E Blues Scale

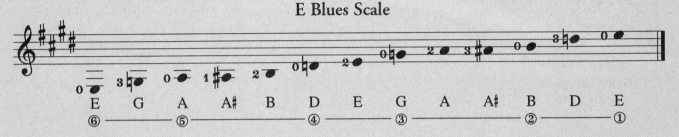

The lyrics of blues songs traditionally form a three-line stanza, with the second line repeating the first, and the third line rhyming.

> *When we sing the blues, we sing 'em all day long,*
> *When we sing the blues, we sing 'em all day long,*
> *When we sing the blues, it makes us feel so strong.*

Three four-measure phrases of music accompany the three lines of the stanza. This is often referred to as the 12-bar (12-measure) blues form. The time signature is usually $\frac{4}{4}$, with the I, IV, and V chords being used to create the accompaniment. The chords of the blues can be varied in many ways, such as by making them seventh chords.

Playing the Blues

1. Play the 12-bar chord progression below in the keys of G Major, A Major, and E Major, using the I, IV, and V7 chords as indicated. Play a downstroke on each beat of each measure. Play V7 instead of I in the last measure if you repeat to the beginning of the form.

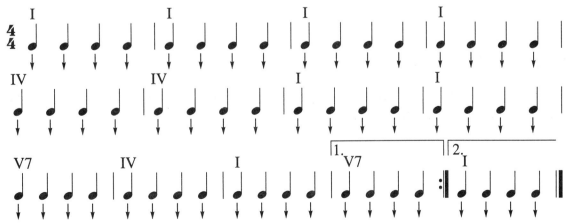

2. Play the E Blues scale. Then, use the notes of the scale to improvise **riffs**, which are short, repeated melodic patterns, often one measure in length.

3. Improvise riffs based on the E Blues scale while a partner or the rest of the class plays the blues chord progression in E.

Teacher Tips, Student page 67:

- *Sing the Blues* is in the key of E Major. It is a "prototype" 12-bar blues form.

- Remind students to "swing" the eighth notes.

- The chords in *Sing the Blues* are the E Major chords, on student page 48.

Warm-up, Student page 67:

- Review with students eighth note triplets on student page 58. Have students perform *Habanera*, listening to the feeling of playing triplets.

Activities, Student page 67:

- Review with students the definitions of **eighth note triplet, swing,** and **first and second endings** provided on student page 67.

- Play recordings of swing for students, and ask them to listen for the triplet feel of the music.

- Have students complete a clapping exercise to better understand the feel of swing. Divide the class into two groups, and have one group clap steady, eighth note triplets. Have the other group clap the quarter note/eighth note triplet found in swing music. To better hear the differences between the two rhythms, have the group clapping the quarter note/eighth note triplet play the rhythm on an open string. Switch roles and repeat the exercise.

- Review with students the instructions for playing *Sing the Blues* in class.

- Rehearse the melody of *Sing the Blues* with students in class. When students feel comfortable with the melody, sing the words along with them as they play, or have the students sing while they play. Then add the chords and bass lines.

- Divide the class into groups of three. Assign each student a part, so that each group has a student playing the melody, chords, and bass. Explain to students that those playing the bass line should experiment with playing other tones from the E Major scale and the E Blues scale on beats 2, 3, and 4. Beat 1 is reserved for playing the bass tone for the chord indicated. Switch roles and repeat until each student has had the opportunity to improvise on the bass line.

- Have students write new verses for *Sing the Blues* together in class. Or, have volunteers compose their own verses and then sing their verses while others accompany them on the guitar.

- Have students improvise **fills** with tones from the E Blues scale on the long, tied notes in *Sing the Blues*.

- For more advanced students, encourage them to compose their own 12-bar blues melody, and perform it for the class.

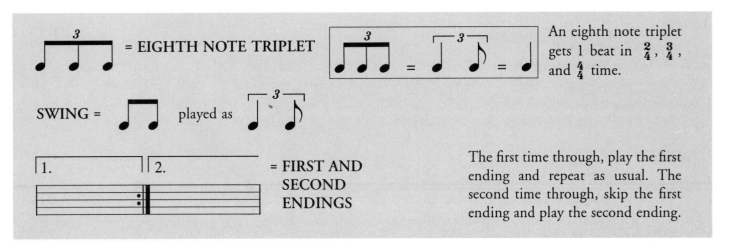

 Sing the Blues

MELODY	Swing all of the eighth notes ( ). During the long tied tones at the end of each four-measure phrase, improvise **fills** (fill-in melodies) with tones from the E Blues scale. To allow for more opportunities to improvise, repeat the piece. On the second time through, replace the original melody with an improvised melody based on the E Blues scale, and on rhythms from the piece.
CHORDS	Accent the second and fourth beats of the measure. Strum:
BASS	Play the bass tone to the chord on the first beat of each measure. If you are the only bass line player, experiment with other tones from the E Major scale and the E Blues scale on beats 2, 3, and 4.

Sing the Blues

Grant Gustafson

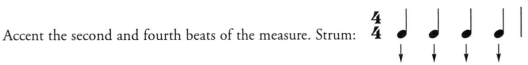

When we sing the blues,— we sing 'em all day long.———— When we

sing the blues,— we sing 'em all day long.———— When we

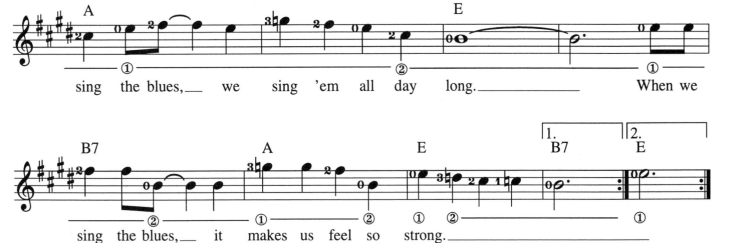

sing the blues,— it makes us feel so strong.————

Teacher Tips, Student pages 68–71:

• *St. Louis Blues* will challenge students to use many of the skills they have learned thus far in the book.

• *St. Louis Blues*, by W.C. Handy, is a prototype of the extended 12-bar blues form. It has five sections:

A – 12-bar blues form in the key of A Major

B – 16 bars in the key of A Minor

C – 12-bar blues form in the key of A Major

A – 12-bar blues form in the key of A Major

D – coda

A and C have different melodies. *St. Louis Blues* makes use of the E Blues scale, introduced on student page 66.

• Because of the complexity of this piece, plan to spend several class periods rehearsing and working on the rhythms, chords, and improvisational aspects of the work.

• While students are learning *St. Louis Blues,* plan to continue rehearsing the music for the final recital at the end of each class period and/or in joint rehearsals with all of your guitar classes.

Warm-up, Student pages 68–71:

• Have students play the melody of *Sing the Blues* in unison to reinforce how to swing eighth notes.

Activities, Student pages 68–71:

• Have students write in the left hand fingerings for the melody of *St. Louis Blues* in I Position.

• Play the A Minor Pentatonic scale in V Position with students. Students should not be playing any open strings.

• Review the instructions for playing *St. Louis Blues* provided on student page 68.

• Review with students how to swing eighth notes.

• Have students note that the first measure uses a I7 (A7) and the second measure uses a IV7 (D7). This is typical of a blues progression. Students can refer to student page 27 for a reminder of how to play the D7 chord, and to student page 38 for a reminder of how to play the A7 chord.

• Have students identify the blue notes.

• Remind students to dampen the eighth note rests.

• Have students identify the syncopations before they play. Ask students to identify which weak beats are stressed.

• Rehearse the melody for *St. Louis Blues* together as a class. As a result of the complex rhythms in *St. Louis Blues*, students may have difficulty playing together, particularly when swinging eighth notes. Students may benefit by practicing the piece as a homework assignment.

• If students are having difficult playing the syncopation, have them try playing the melody without syncopations and listening to the difference.

- Once students feel comfortable with the melody, rehearse the chords and bass lines together as a class. Make sure that students continue to swing eighth notes.

- Have students improvise using the A Minor Pentatonic scale during the long, tied notes. Students may benefit from working on improvising on the A Minor Pentatonic scale as a homework assignment.

- Have students develop simple riffs that can be repeated during the melody.

- Have some students sing the words while others play, or encourage students to sing the words as they play.

- If you have a recording of *St. Louis Blues* by W.C. Handy, share it with students. Listening to the recording at the beginning of each class period during which *St. Louis Blues* will be rehearsed will help students in their own performance of the work.

- After students have mastered *St. Louis Blues*, duplicate and distribute the Evaluation Worksheet on page 159. Divide students into groups of five. Ask each student to perform the two-octave E Blues scale and the melody of *St. Louis Blues*. Have the other students in the group evaluate the performer based on the criteria provided on the worksheet.

- Complete the Unit 14 Review checklist on student page 71.

Interdisciplinary Studies, Student pages 68–71:

- Read the following historical information on W.C. Handy to students:

Known as the "Father of the Blues," W.C. Handy (1873–1958) was an accomplished trumpeter, band director, music publisher, and composer of blues and spirituals. Handy was a pioneer in introducing the blues, originally an African-American music style, to the general American public. He did this by composing and publishing songs, like *Memphis Blues* (1912) and *St. Louis Blues* (1914), which appealed to a wider audience. He also published the work of many other African-American composers, and funded concerts of African-American music, from work songs to orchestral works.

Units 13 & 14 Quiz, Student pages 68–71:

- The duplicable Units 13 & 14 Quiz is provided on page 157. The Units 13 & 14 Quiz asks students to identify the E Blues and E Minor Pentatonic scales, the 12-bar blues chord progression, and blues-related terminology.

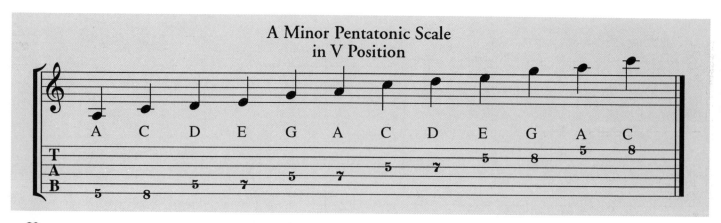

A Minor Pentatonic Scale in V Position

 St. Louis Blues

St. Louis Blues is divided into three sections. The first (measures 1–12) is in A Major and follows the 12-bar blues form. The second (measures 13–28) is in A Minor. The final section (measures 29–52) is again in A Major with the 12-bar blues form appearing twice.

MELODY Swing all of the eighth notes. Use the A Minor Pentatonic Scale to improvise fills during the long tied tones. On the second time through, replace the original melody with an improvised melody based on the A Minor Pentatonic scale and rhythms from the piece.

CHORDS The chord line in the middle shows you both the chords and the strum rhythm to be used. Swing all of the eighth notes.

BASS Play the bass line as written. Swing all of the eighth notes.

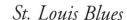

St. Louis Blues

W.C. Handy (1873–1958)
arr. Grant Gustafson

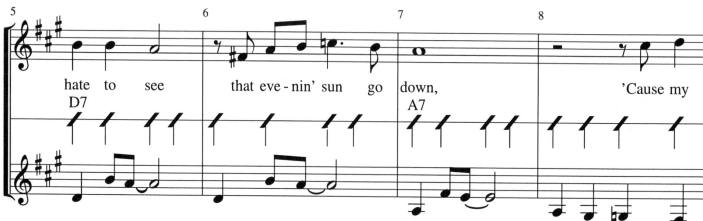

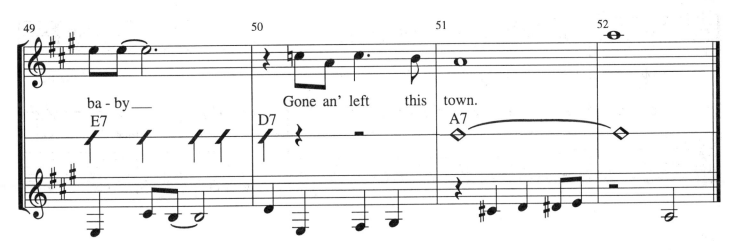

Unit 14 Review

Identify:
- ☐ blues
- ☐ E Blues scale
- ☐ 12-bar blues form
- ☐ riff
- ☐ swing
- ☐ fill
- ☐ A Minor Pentatonic scale

Perform:
- ☐ *Sing the Blues*
- ☐ *St. Louis Blues*

Teacher Tips, Student page 72:

- Students can be introduced to tuning their own guitars at any point in the course that seems appropriate. In order to tune the open ⑤ string, a piano/keyboard, tuning fork, electronic tuner, or pitch pipe will be required to serve as a reference. The tuning activity on student page 72 should be completed in class. Encourage students to tune their own guitars when practicing at home.

- Possibly the greatest cause of consternation in class guitar is to keep all the guitars in tune. While the ultimate goal is to lead students to effectively tune their own instruments, the development of this skill takes time, and many students will still be unable to do so at the end of the course. Be aware of the strengths and weaknesses of each student, and help those who are having difficulty tuning. To ensure a successful and gratifying music-making experience, guitars must be tuned to the same pitch.

- Students should be encouraged to learn to tune their instruments through relating the strings to one another (as provided on student page 72). This will help them develop aural skills to be able to tune their guitars outside of class, and to check their instruments during class time.

- The tone given by a tuning fork (A = 440 Hertz) can be found on the guitar, either on the ① string (high E string) at the 5th fret, or as a harmonic tone on the ⑤ string above the 5th fret. Harmonic tones on the guitar are produced when the left hand fingertip gently touches above a fret and then quickly releases, allowing the entire string to vibrate. The strongest harmonic tones are found above the 5th, 7th, and 12th frets.

Activities, Student page 72:

- Have students explore the fingerboard by searching for and identifying the same notes in different positions and on different strings. Identify the pitches of the harmonic tones at the 5th, 7th, and 12th frets.

- For individual tuning, have all guitars pre-tuned at the beginning of each day. Then, at the beginning of each class session, go around the room to each student and compare the students' guitar strings individually with those of your guitar, beginning with the ① string (high E). Play alternating rest strokes in a slow, steady beat.

- For group tuning, conduct a "tuning session" with your class once all guitars have been individually tuned. This will ensure that all guitars are tuned in unison, will create a full sound by having all guitars playing at the same time, and will demand the attention of each individual. Beginning on the ① string, a conductor (teacher or student) should give a steady beat with the right hand. All guitarists should carefully follow this beat and play alternating rest strokes on the ① string. While the guitars are playing in unison, listen for which guitars may sound out of tune and make corrections. The conductor should signal when to change to the next-lowest string, maintaining a steady beat. This tuning session can be enhanced by using different meters and rhythms and by playing gradually faster and gradually slower.

TUNING THE STRINGS

Finding the correct pitches for tuning the guitar strings can be done in several ways. The guitar can be tuned to the piano, as indicated in the diagram on page 5. Many musicians also have a tuning fork or pitch pipe that can provide the correct pitches for the guitar strings.

The strings of the guitar can also be tuned by comparing the same notes on different strings. Using the diagram for reference, follow the steps below to tune your guitar by comparing notes.

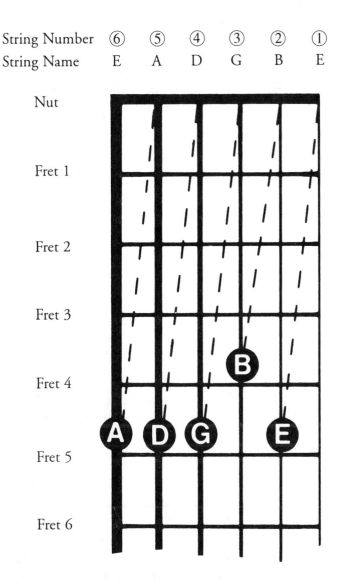

1. The open ⑤ string must be tuned to the piano, a tuning fork, or other tuning device.

2. Press behind the 5th fret on the ⑥ string and play. Then, immediately afterward, play the open ⑤ string. If the ⑥ string sounds higher or lower, adjust the tuning machines to match the pitch played on the ⑤ string.

3. Tune the open ④ string to the 5th fret on the ⑤ string.

4. Tune the open ③ string to the 5th fret on the ④ string.

5. Tune the open ② string to the 4th fret on the ③ string.

6. Tune the open ① string to the 5th fret on the ② string.

WORKSHEET 1
Correlated with Student pages 2–3

A Brief History of the Guitar

Name _____

The Early Guitars (1450–1800) were small, often elaborately ornamented instruments with 4 to 6 pairs (courses) of gut strings. Melodies were plucked and chords were strummed. They were favored both by the royal courts of Europe and the musicians of the street. Spanish explorers brought guitars with them to the New World, where they spread throughout the entire hemisphere.
Guitarists: 16th century: Luis de Milán (Spain); 17th c: Francesco Corbetta (Italy), Robert de Visée (France), Gaspar Sanz (Spain); 18th c: Benjamin Franklin (America).

The Classic Guitar (1800–present), with its 6 single strings, is played with the fingers and produces a warm, full sound. Nylon strings replaced gut in the 1940's. Music from the past five centuries, encompassing a multitude of musical styles, is played on the classic guitar.
Guitarists & Composers: 19th c: Mauro Giuliani (Italy), Fernando Sor (Spain), Madame Sydney Pratten (England); early 20th c: Francisco Tárrega (Spain), Heitor Villa-Lobos (Brazil); late 20th c: Eduardo Falú (Argentina), John Williams (Australia), Liona Boyd (Canada), Kazuhito Yamashita (Japan), Julian Bream (England), Leo Brouwer (Cuba), Eliot Fisk (USA).

The Flamenco Guitar (1800–present) is a nylon-string acoustic guitar that is used to play the flamenco music of Spain. This intensely emotional music is characterized by loud and fast chord, melody, and percussive playing on the guitar. It is often used to accompany flamenco dancers and singers.
Guitarists: Ramon Montoya (Spain), Ottmar Liebert (Germany).

The Western Guitar (1900–present) became a distinct member of the guitar family when steel strings and a more robust construction were introduced. It became an instrument of popular music and the new, bright sound was ideal for the blues, bluegrass and folk finger-picking styles, and country. It is played either with fingers or with a plectrum. Different cultures throughout the world have adapted the western guitar to play their own music.
Guitarists: Gene Autry, Elvis Presley, Elizabeth Cotten, Bob Dylan, Mary Chapin Carpenter, Joan Baez, Judy Collins.

The 12-String Acoustic Guitar (1920–present) has 6 courses of steel strings. It is used to play blues, rock, and folk and is played with a plectrum or with the fingers. Often, a slide (bottleneck) is used to create a "whiney" effect.
Guitarists: Blind Willie McTell, George Harrison.

The Hollow Body Electric Guitar (1930–present) developed directly from the first attempts to amplify an acoustic guitar. Its mellow sound is preferred by jazz guitarists.
Guitarists: Herb Ellis, Barney Kessel, Charlie Christian, Wes Montgomery, Chet Atkins, Tracy Chapman.

The Solid Body Electric Guitar (1940–present) was invented to prevent unwanted feedback from amplified acoustic guitars. It has a direct tone and is the favorite of rock and blues guitarists. This type of guitar allows for innumerable special effects through electronic means.
Guitarists: Jimmy Page, David Gilmour, Frank Zappa, Jerry Garcia, Carlos Santana.

WORKSHEET 2
Correlated with Student page 11

Name _____

A. Write in the correct time signature for the following examples. With your class, play each line on a single open string using the alternating rest stroke.

1)

2)

3)

B. Using quarter, half, and whole notes, compose your own rhythms in the following time signatures.

4) **3/4** | | | ‖

5) **2/4** | | | ‖

6) **4/4** | | | ‖

C. Listen to a partner, or your teacher, as they play their compositions from section B. First, identify the time signature and beat, then write down the rhythms in the appropriate blank measures below.

4) **3/4** | | | ‖

5) **2/4** | | | ‖

6) **4/4** | | | ‖

WORKSHEET 3
Correlated with Student page 12

Name _____

A. Practice drawing treble clefs, whole notes, half notes, and quarter notes in the staffs below.

   1) Draw four treble clefs.
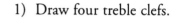

   2) Draw four whole notes.

   3) Draw four half notes.

   4) Draw four quarter notes.

B. Study the letter names of the notes shown. Then, write in the letter names of the notes in the blanks provided beneath each note on the staff below.

F   A   C   E

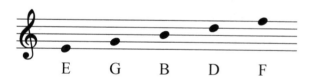

E   G   B   D   F

_____ _____ _____ _____   _____ _____ _____ _____

C. Fill in the TAB for the notes below. Since each note is an open string on the guitar, write an "0" on the appropriate line of the TAB.

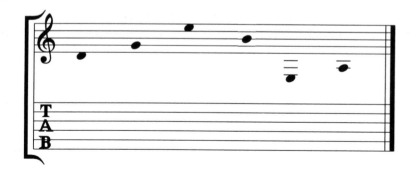

WORKSHEET 4
Correlated with Student page 18

Name _____

A. Compose two-tone melodies of four measures each, using combinations of ♩ ♩ , ♩ and ♩ .
   Pay attention to the time signatures indicated.

   1) On the ③ string with the tones G and A:

   2) On the ② string with the tones B and D:

   3) On the ① string with the tones E and G:

B1. Listen carefully to a classmate, or to your teacher, as he or she plays the compositions completed in
    section A. Write down the rhythms that you hear in the blank measures below.

   1) **2/4**

   2) **3/4**

   3) **4/4**

B2. The classmate or teacher will play his or her compositions again. First, have the performer play the
    two notes that are included in the composition. Then, listen for the pattern of the two notes played,
    and write down H each time the higher of the two notes is played, and L each time the lower of the
    two notes is played. For this exercise, the rhythm will not be notated, only the pattern of higher and
    lower notes.

   1) _____

   2) _____

   3) _____

WORKSHEET 5

Correlated with Student page 32

Name _____

A. Insert the bar lines, and write in the counting. Then, play each exercise with your class.

1)

2)

B. Compose a four-measure melody in ⁶⁄₈ time, using the tones G (③ open), B (② open), and D (②, 3rd fret). The last note has been completed for you. Use the following rhythmic combinations:

C1. Listen carefully to a classmate, or to your teacher, as he or she plays the composition completed in section B. Write down the rhythms that you hear in the blank measures below.

C2. The classmate or teacher will play his or her composition again. First, have the performer play the three notes that are included in the composition. Then, listen for the pattern of the three notes played, and write down H each time the highest of the three notes is played, M each time the middle note is played, and L each time the lowest note is played. For this exercise, the rhythm will not be notated, only the pattern of high, middle, and low notes.

_____

WORKSHEET 6

Correlated with Student page 53

Introduction to Chord Structure

Name _____

A **CHORD** is three or more tones played as a unit. These tones may appear in any order, although it is common for the root of the chord to be in the bass. Chord tones may also appear more than once in a chord. For this reason, there are many possible ways of playing any one chord.

A chord can be constructed on any tone in a scale by playing every other note. The interval between these notes is a **MAJOR THIRD** (two whole steps) or a **MINOR THIRD** (one whole step and one half step).

Study the examples of major and minor chords below. Notice that the distance between the **ROOT** (the note that corresponds with the letter name of the chord) and the note a third above the root (the **THIRD** of the chord) determines whether the chord is major or minor. The top tone is the same in both major and minor chord structures.

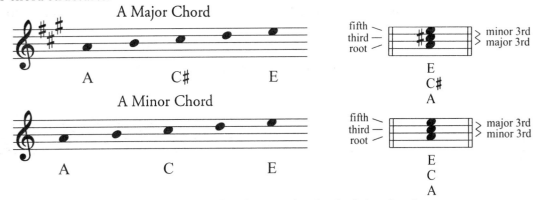

You can change a chord from major to minor by altering the third of the chord.

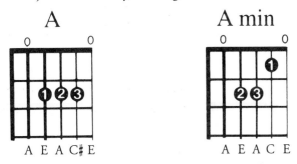

Additional tones can be added to a chord. The "7" behind a chord refers to a **SEVENTH CHORD**. A seventh chord can be created by adding another third to a chord constructed on the major scale. In a seventh chord, the interval between the root and the top note is a seventh. The parts of a seventh chord are known as the root, third, fifth, and seventh. The more important seventh chord in a major key is a V7 chord. Called a **DOMINANT SEVENTH CHORD**, the V7 chord consists of a major chord with a minor third on top. The dominant seventh chord is written with a 7 next to the root letter name in order to signify the seventh chord.

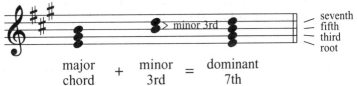

WORKSHEET 7
Correlated with Student page 66

Blues Composition
in Three Easy Steps

Name _____

1) Compose a three-line verse. Model your verse after the three-line stanza on page 66. The first and second lines should be identical, and the last word of the third line should rhyme with the first and second line. The three lines will be labeled A A B.

A _____

A _____

B _____

2) In the spaces provided above the staff lines below, write in the chords for the 12-bar blues form in E Major.

A

A1

B

3) Attach tones of the E Blues scale and rhythmic values to the syllables of the three-line verse that you have composed. Important syllables should be longer, others should be shorter. Fit each line into the first three measures of each four-measure group, with the last word falling in the third measure. Remember to assign rhythmic values to the words so that four beats occur in each measure. Perform your composition for your class.

INTRODUCING: THE GUITAR!

Unit 1 Quiz

Name _____

A. Match the numbered parts of the guitar in the diagram with the correct names in the list below.

_____ soundboard
_____ frets
_____ back
_____ saddle
_____ tuning machines
_____ head
_____ fingerboard
_____ rosette
_____ nut
_____ strings
_____ neck
_____ soundhole
_____ bridge
_____ sides

B. Match the type of guitar with a style associated with it. Each style may have more than one guitar associated with it.

15) Electric guitar (solid body)   _____ Spanish
16) Flamenco guitar   _____ Blues
17) Classic guitar   _____ Rock
18) Electric guitar (hollow body)   _____ Folk
19) Western guitar   _____ Jazz
20) 12-String guitar   _____ Latin American

C. Name a guitarist that plays (or played) each of the above types of guitar:

15) _____   18) _____
16) _____   19) _____
17) _____   20) _____

D. Fill in the letter names of the open strings of the guitar in the diagram of a guitar neck below.

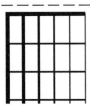

CREATING TONES & READING MUSIC

Units 2 & 3 Quiz

Name _____

A. Fill in the letter names of the fingers of the right hand.

B. In the blank measures below, compose rhythms using ♩ , 𝅗𝅥 , 𝅗𝅥. , and 𝅝 . Before composing, note the time signature for each line.

1) **2/4**

2) **3/4**

3) **4/4**

C. At the beginning of the blank staff below, draw in a treble clef and a time signature of your choice (2/4 , 3/4 , or 4/4). Using the rhythms you composed in the same time signature in section B, above, create a four-measure composition by assigning each note value a pitch on the open ①, ②, and ③ strings in the blank staff. Remember to draw in bar lines and fill in the TAB.

T
A
B

D. Play your composition for the class. Remember to count the beats carefully, accent the first note of each measure, and play with the alternating rest stroke.

CHANGING PITCH

Unit 4 Quiz

Name _____

A. Fill in the numbers of the fingers of the left hand.

B. Complete the following measures using these rhythms: ♩ ♩ and ♩ . Each blank will either hold

 or ♩ .

C. Fill in the TAB for the notes in the staff below. Write in the names of the notes.

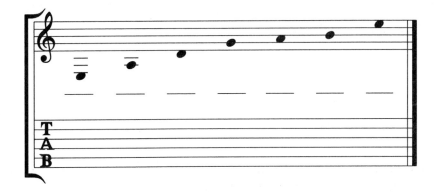

FIRST SONGS

Unit 5 Quiz

Name _____

A. Complete the measures below using 𝄽 , ▬ , or ▬ rest values. Remember that a whole rest indicates the duration of a measure, whether the time signature is $\frac{2}{4}$, $\frac{3}{4}$, or $\frac{4}{4}$. Fill in one rest per blank.

B. Insert bar lines, and write in the counting.

C. In the blank measures below, compose a short rhythm exercise using each of the following notes and rests at least once: ♪ ♩ ♩. 𝅗𝅥 𝄽 ▬

6) $\frac{4}{4}$

D. Study the music example below. Then answer the following questions:

7) What is the time signature? _____

8) What is the highest note in the song? _____

9) What is the lowest note in the song? _____

10) What is the shortest note in the song? _____

11) What is the longest note in the song? _____

12) How many different pitches are there? _____

London Bridge

MAKING MUSIC: G MAJOR

Unit 6 Quiz

Name _____

A. Write in the names of the notes below, and then draw the notes which fall an octave above each of the given notes.

B. In the staff below, fill in the correct key signature to make this series of notes the G Major scale. Then, name the notes, and circle the pairs of notes which are a half step apart.

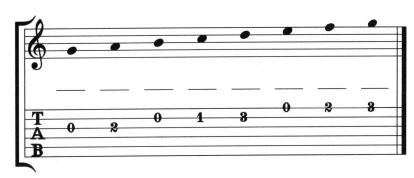

C. Name the notes, and circle the pairs of notes which are a half step apart.

D. Name the I, IV, and V7 chords in the key of G Major.

_____   _____   _____

        I   IV   V7

E. In the statements below, circle the correct word in each pair of underlined words to make each statement true.

1) A sharp before a note tells you to raise/lower the pitch by a half step. You do this by moving up/down one fret on the fingerboard.

2) A flat before a note tells you to raise/lower the pitch by a half step. You do this by moving up/down one fret on the fingerboard.

MAKING MUSIC: G MAJOR

Unit 6 Quiz, continued

Name _____

F. Insert bar lines to create the pick-up values indicated.

3) One quarter note pick-up

4) Two quarter notes pick-up

5) Two eighth notes pick-up

G. Match the following terms with their definitions:

6) *p (piano)*
7) *f (forte)*
8) *dim. (diminuendo)*
9) *cresc. (crescendo)*

_____ become gradually softer
_____ soft
_____ loud
_____ become gradually louder

H. In the blank measures below, compose a rhythm exercise in 6/8 time. Use each of the following rhythms at least once: ♩. and ♪♪♪ .

10)

I. Complete the following measures with ♪, 𝄽, or ▬ . Fill in one rest per blank.

11)

12)

13)

MAKING MUSIC: C MAJOR

Unit 7 Quiz

Name _____

A. In the blank staff and TAB below, indicate the C Major key signature. Then, write out the one-octave C Major scale. Write in the names of the notes between the staff and TAB, and fill in the TAB for each note. When you have completed the scale, circle the pairs of notes which are a half step apart.

B. Name the I, IV, and V7 chords in the key of C Major.

_____   _____   _____
        I   IV   V7

C. Name the notes and fill in the TAB below. Then, circle the pairs of notes which are a half step apart.

D. Add a sharp, flat, or natural to the second note in each pair of notes below to make the interval either a half step or a whole step, as indicated.

1) whole step

2) half step

3) whole step

4) whole step

Making Music: D Major

Unit 8 Quiz

Name _____

A. In the blank staff and TAB below, indicate the D Major key signature. Then, write out the one-octave D Major scale. Write in the names of the notes between the staff and TAB, and fill in the TAB for each note. When you have completed the scale, circle the pairs of notes which are a half step apart.

B. Name the I, IV, and V7 chords in the key of D Major.

_____   _____   _____

          I   IV   V7

C. The blanks in the following measures require either 4 sixteenth notes or 1 sixteenth note to complete the measures. For each numbered blank, write in "4" or "1" in the spaces below.

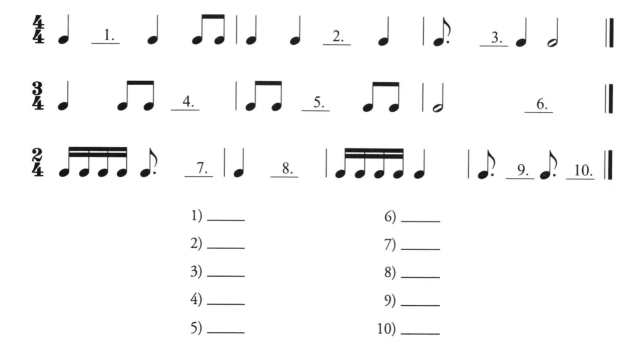

    1) _____   6) _____

    2) _____   7) _____

    3) _____   8) _____

    4) _____   9) _____

    5) _____   10) _____

MAKING MUSIC: C MAJOR

Unit 7 Quiz

Name _____

A. In the blank staff and TAB below, indicate the C Major key signature. Then, write out the one-octave C Major scale. Write in the names of the notes between the staff and TAB, and fill in the TAB for each note. When you have completed the scale, circle the pairs of notes which are a half step apart.

B. Name the I, IV, and V7 chords in the key of C Major.

_____   _____   _____

     I   IV   V7

C. Name the notes and fill in the TAB below. Then, circle the pairs of notes which are a half step apart.

D. Add a sharp, flat, or natural to the second note in each pair of notes below to make the interval either a half step or a whole step, as indicated.

1) whole step

2) half step

3) whole step

4) whole step

MAKING MUSIC: D MAJOR

Unit 8 Quiz

Name _____

A. In the blank staff and TAB below, indicate the D Major key signature. Then, write out the one-octave D Major scale. Write in the names of the notes between the staff and TAB, and fill in the TAB for each note. When you have completed the scale, circle the pairs of notes which are a half step apart.

B. Name the I, IV, and V7 chords in the key of D Major.

_____   _____   _____

I   IV   V7

C. The blanks in the following measures require either 4 sixteenth notes or 1 sixteenth note to complete the measures. For each numbered blank, write in "4" or "1" in the spaces below.

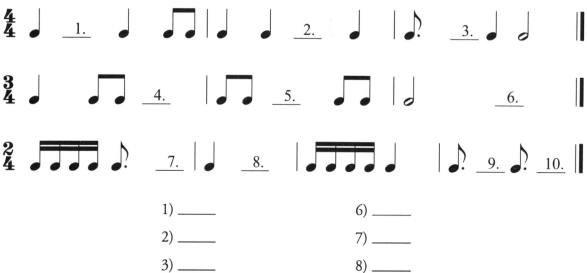

1) _____   6) _____

2) _____   7) _____

3) _____   8) _____

4) _____   9) _____

5) _____   10) _____

MAKING MUSIC: A MAJOR

Unit 9 Quiz

Name _____

A. In the blank staff and TAB below, indicate the A Major key signature. Then, write out the one-octave A Major scale. Write in the names of the notes between the staff and TAB, and fill in the TAB for each note. When you have completed the scale, circle the pairs of notes which are a half step apart.

B. Name the I, IV, and V7 chords in the key of A Major.

_____   _____   _____
       I   IV   V7

C. Write in the guitar fingerings to the following notes in I Position. The encircled string numbers should be below the note, and the left hand finger numbers to the left of the note.

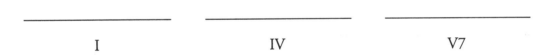

D. Insert bar lines, and write in the counting.

E. Complete the measures below with ♩, 𝅗𝅥 or ♪ .

F. In the statements below, circle the correct word in each pair of underlined words to make each statement true.

1) A sound that is tense and unstable is called a <u>consonance/dissonance</u>.

2) A sound that is stable and free of tension is called a <u>consonance/dissonance</u>.

BEYOND THE MAJOR BASICS: E MAJOR

Unit 10 Quiz

Name _____

A. Identify the major keys for each of the following key signatures. Then complete the major scale and label the notes in the scale for each major key.

____ 1)

____ 2)

____ 3)

____ 4)

____ 5)

B. Name the I, IV, and V7 chords in the following major keys.

	I	IV	V7
6) C Major	_____	_____	_____
7) G Major	_____	_____	_____
8) D Major	_____	_____	_____
9) A Major	_____	_____	_____
10) E Major	_____	_____	_____

C. In the following rhythm, create syncopations by transferring a natural accent from a strong beat to a weak beat by using ties.

A CHANGE OF MOOD: A MINOR

Unit 11 Quiz

Name _____

A. Identify the following scales as being the A Major scale, A Natural Minor scale, A Harmonic Minor scale, or ascending A Melodic Minor scale. Name the notes and circle pairs of notes which are a half step apart.

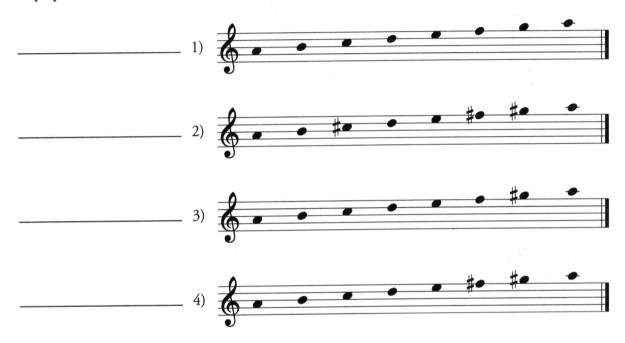

_____ 1)

_____ 2)

_____ 3)

_____ 4)

B. Name the i, iv, and V7 chords in the key of A Minor.

_____   _____   _____

    i   iv   V7

C. Write in the guitar fingerings to the following notes in I Position. The encircled string numbers should be below the note, and the left hand finger numbers to the left of the note.

5)

A CHANGE OF MOOD: E MINOR

Unit 12 Quiz

Name _____

A. Identify the following scales as being the E Major scale, E Natural Minor scale, E Harmonic Minor scale, or ascending E Melodic Minor scale. Name the notes and circle pairs of notes which are a half step apart.

_____ 1)

_____ 2)

_____ 3)

_____ 4)

B. Name the i, iv, and V7 chords in the key of E Minor.

_____   _____   _____
i   iv   V7

C. Insert bar lines.

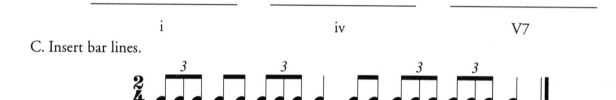

D. Complete the following equations by matching rhythms in column A to rhythms in column B. Rhythms that are "equal" have the same number of beats in $\frac{4}{4}$ time.

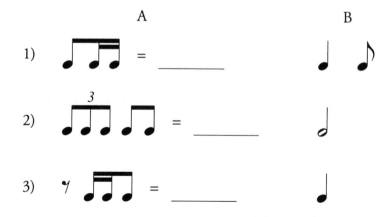

THE PENTATONIC SCALE & THE BLUES

Units 13 & 14 Quiz

Name _____

A. Insert the "blue note" into the following E Minor Pentatonic scale to create the E Blues scale.

B. In the blank measures below, write in the chords for the basic 12-bar blues form in the key of G Major. One chord will appear per measure.

C. In your own words, define the following terms:

1) improvisation _____

_____

2) riff _____

_____

3) fill _____

_____

4) blues _____

_____

5) swing _____

_____

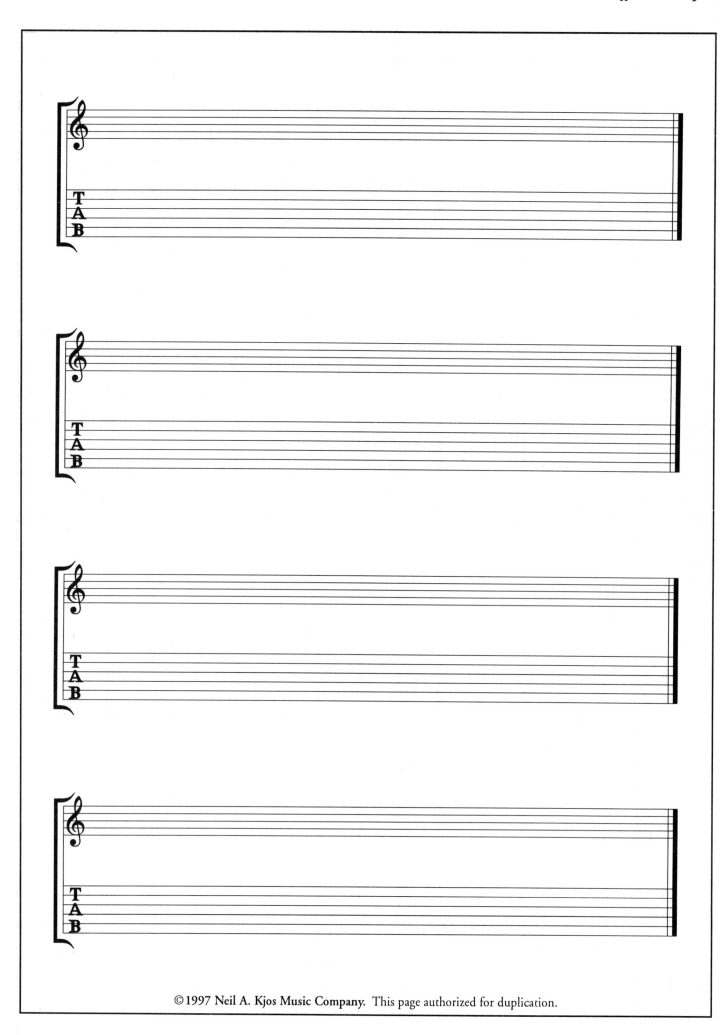

EVALUATION WORKSHEET

Name _____

Evaluate your classmates' performance of the scale, chord progression, and musical selection by grading them on a scale of 1 to 3 on each of the criteria provided.

1 = Fair;   2 = Good;   3 = Excellent

Scale:	Chord Progression:	Musical Selection:
Name _____ ___ Accuracy ___ Finger placement ___ Playing position/posture ___ Alternating rest stroke Overall: ___ /36	___ Strum technique ___ Playing position ___ Finger placement ___ Smooth transition between chords	___ Rhythm/steady beat ___ Notes ___ Time signature ___ Musical expression
Name _____ ___ Accuracy ___ Finger placement ___ Playing position/posture ___ Alternating rest stroke Overall: ___ /36	___ Strum technique ___ Playing position ___ Finger placement ___ Smooth transition between chords	___ Rhythm/steady beat ___ Notes ___ Time signature ___ Musical expression
Name _____ ___ Accuracy ___ Finger placement ___ Playing position/posture ___ Alternating rest stroke Overall: ___ /36	___ Strum technique ___ Playing position ___ Finger placement ___ Smooth transition between chords	___ Rhythm/steady beat ___ Notes ___ Time signature ___ Musical expression
Name _____ ___ Accuracy ___ Finger placement ___ Playing position/posture ___ Alternating rest stroke Overall: ___ /36	___ Strum technique ___ Playing position ___ Finger placement ___ Smooth transition between chords	___ Rhythm/steady beat ___ Notes ___ Time signature ___ Musical expression

MUSIC THEORY INDEX

Music Theory Terminology Introduced		Teacher Page	Student Page as appears in Teacher's Edition	Correlated Student Page in Student Edition
bar line		20	21	10
beat		20	21	10
chord		42	43	21
chord chart		42	43	21
chord progression		54	55	27
clef, treble		24	25	12
consonance		88	90	45
dissonance		88	90	45
dynamics		60	62	30
	diminuendo/crescendo	60	62	30
	forte/piano	60	62	30
first and second endings		128	129	67
flat		52	53	26
improvisation		122	123	64
interval		52	53	26
key, major		52	53	26
key signature		52	53	26
ledger lines		24	25	12
measure		20	21	10
natural		74	75	37
note		20	21	10
	dotted eighth	82	83	41
	dotted eighth/sixteenth combination	82	83	41
	dotted half	26	27	13
	dotted quarter	50	51	25
	eighth	36	37	18
	eighth note triplet	112	113	58
	eighth/sixteenth combination	114	115	59
	half	20	21	10
	pick-up	56	57	28
	quarter	20	21	10
	sixteenth	80	81	40
	whole	20	21	10
octave		52	53	26
repeat sign		26	27	13
rest		48	49	24
	eighth	66	67	33
	half/quarter/whole	48	49	24
scale		52	53	26
	A Major	86	87	43
	A Minor	102	104	53
	A Minor Pentatonic	130	132	68
	blues	126	127	66
	C Major	68	69	34
	D Major	76	77	38
	E Blues	126	127	66
	E Major	94	95	48
	E Minor	110	111	57
	E Minor Pentatonic	122	123	64
	G Major	54	55	27
	major	52	53	26
	minor	102	103	52
	pentatonic	122	123	64
sharp		52	53	26
staff notation		24	25	12
step, whole/half		52	53	26
swing		128	129	67
syncopation		98	100	50
tablature		24	25	12
tie		40	41	20
time signature		20	21	10
	5/4	88	89	44
	6/8	64	65	32
	2/4, 3/4, 4/4	20	21	10